ISBN 0-9722332-4-5
Published by MotiVision Media
http://www.motivisionmedia.com

Book website, related seminars, and ordering information:
http://www.yourbestpersonalstyle.com
email: kimdehaven@cox.net
First edition: April 2008

MotiVision Media

Authors: Kim DeHaven with Ruth Milliron and Bette DeHaven
Content Editor and Writer–Beka Patterson
Cover Design–MotiVision Media
Layout and Graphics–MotiVision Media

A Recipe for
your Best
Personal Style

MotiVision Media • California • 2008

We dedicate this book

...to women everywhere. You're beautiful on the inside AND out and we treasure the gifts and lessons you've given us. Thank you to Beka Patterson. Without you, this book would have never happened. We appreciate you more than you could ever know. Brad DeHaven. Your talents never cease to amaze us. Your determination, drive, and ambition are an inspiration. Finally, to our families. You are our REASON and our motivation. We feel blessed every day.

Table of Contents

ONE . . . . Why a Recipe? 7

TWO . . . . Start from Scratch 11

THREE . . . . Color: The Essential Ingredient 19

FOUR . . . . Toss it Up 31

FIVE . . . . Prep Time 39

SIX . . . . The Frosting on the Cake 51

SEVEN . . . . The Secret Ingredient 67

EIGHT . . . . What's Your Flavor? 87

NINE . . . . Spice it Up 107

TEN . . . . What's in the Pantry? 123

ELEVEN . . . . Shopping List 129

TWELVE . . . . Microwave Style 137

THIRTEEN . . . . Just Like Wine, Better with Time 143

FOURTEEN . . . . The Final Course 151

Kim DeHaven has a degree in interior design. Her flare for style led her into the field of personal image. Kim has not only created an extensive image business, but has also taught seminars throughout North America on make-up application, color, and personal style. Her most important roles are that of wife and mother of three young children. Kim lives in San Diego, California.

Ruth Milliron owned and operated a full image salon for 15 years. She is a personal style expert who believes in the attractiveness of every woman "inside and out." Ruth is a former high school educator and college administrator with a degree in clothing, textile, and design. Her natural sense of style and her love for fashion has driven her desire to teach image principles to thousands of women nationwide. She has over 30 years experience as a color and image consultant and personal shopper. Ruth resides in Bowling Green, Ohio.

Bette DeHaven has over 30 years experience in the color and personal image field. She studied clothing, textile, and design in college and has an extensive training background in skin care and make-up application. Her passion is to encourage women to be the best they can be. Bette has authored training materials and conducted weekend seminars for thousands of women around the world. *A Recipe For Your Best Personal Style* is her second book on style and image. Bette is a wife, mother of three, and grandmother of six. She lives in San Diego, California.

Together, these three women present a diverse perspective on why personal style matters and provide a simple recipe every woman can follow to look her very best.

introduction

Have you ever sat in a waiting room, at a busy airport, at the mall, or any place where there were lots of people and just watched? It's fascinating isn't it? We all make assumptions about people simply based on the way they look. You've heard it, just like we have, that you never get a second chance to make a good first impression. How we express ourselves on the outside is like a window facing a busy street with no curtain on it. We've been told that we shouldn't judge a book by its cover, but the real fact is *we do*. Our appearance not only influences how people respond to us but it also influences how we feel, think, act, and respond to others.

I found myself in a daze standing in front of a grilled cheese sandwich I'd just made for my husband. My mind drifted off to the pile of laundry waiting for me, my son's school project, getting a baby sitter for "back to school" night, and five other things on my to-do list. Out of habit, I started cutting the crust off of a grown man's sandwich!

As the mom of three young children, I am constantly getting caught up in the hustle and bustle of school schedules, extra curricular activities, taking care of my home, and helping my husband run a business. There are never enough hours in the day. It seems that we, as moms, are so busy taking care of everyone else that many times we neglect ourselves.

We've all been there. Right before our eyes—laundry piling up, dishes in the sink, and a day ahead filled with obligations and commitments. Wouldn't it be great if you had the time and the know-how to always look good no matter what your day may bring? Well, you're not alone. I'm here to tell you it's doable! You CAN have a great image and only spend a short time doing it. Half the battle is in knowing what to do.

I remember sitting at a volunteer's luncheon as they handed out awards for helping in the kids' class-rooms. They called my name and I went forward to receive my certificate of appreciation. When I sat back down at the table, my girlfriends were whispering to each other. "What?" I said. "You always look so cute. We want to trip you!" I took it as the compliment it was, and we all had a good laugh. I've always been one to want to look my best and I'm thankful that many years ago I learned some simple principles to give me the confidence to have "positive image impact."

I certainly don't spend a lot of time getting ready for things. I simply don't have the time. I do, however, know what styles look best on me, what make-up shades work, and what colors complement my skin tone. It doesn't take a lot of time and money to look and feel great. I urge all of you moms to unite with me! Let's take the little time we do have and pamper ourselves. Trust me, your whole family will benefit.

Kim DeHaven

2

I remember as a little girl, sitting on the bed watching my mom get ready for the day and admiring her peaceful, un-intimidating confidence. She always made an effort to look her best. I never went anywhere with her that she didn't receive a compliment of some sort. My mom wasn't a particularly beautiful woman, but she was beautiful to me. She didn't have a perfect figure; those 20 extra pounds from pregnancy never quite came off. She didn't have a lot of money to spend on clothes and she didn't have a lot of time to fuss with hair and make-up. But what she did have was self-assurance. She didn't focus on being overweight, or not being able to buy designer labels, but on what she could do to successfully dress her body. She learned how to make good clothing choices and to go for "quality not quantity."

I was fortunate to learn these same principles from her, and knowing these things has given me a sense of freedom and confidence as I experience each new stage in life. Right now it happens to be the "everything's going south and I don't think it's coming back" stage. But that's not going to stop me. I'm focused on using every trick in the book, mixing in a little humor, and feeling great at 60 something. So, what's your stage of life? Are you making the most of where you are right now? Or are you focusing on the things that you have no control over?

Mourning the loss of your 20 something waist and longing for smaller thighs, bigger boobs, or longer legs is just a big waste of time and energy. If all you do is focus on the negative, you are missing out on enjoying your life in the moment and you will *never* move forward to a brighter future.

Whether you are 18 or 80, at your goal weight or still working towards it, there is no reason you can't look great. Use *A Recipe For Your Best Personal Style* to learn what it takes to create a great image and start focusing on what you can do to look your best right now. By the time you go through this book, you're going to know how to accentuate what's great and minimize what's not so great. With a few tricks of the trade, you'll be feeling good about yourself and what you have to give others. So . . . don't wait to look great!

 **Ruth Milliron**

Image Matters

On a recent flight to Chicago, I caught the eye of the male flight attendant. As he knelt down beside my seat, I remember thinking, "Wow girl, you've still got it!" It only took a moment for reality to set in and for me to realize I was twice his age. However, he really did notice me and actually wanted to pay me a compliment. He said, "We usually don't see travelers who are dressed so nicely. Thank you." It's compliments like this one that continue to reinforce my belief that style and image really do matter. What I was wearing wasn't anything spectacular, just a comfortable pair of dress pants with a coordinating jacket. The flight attendant may have noticed me because my clothes were neatly pressed, or they were a flattering color for me and had a good fit. Whatever the reason, the fact he thanked me was very telling.

We all love compliments! How would it make you feel if you were to receive compliments on a regular basis? If you're like me, I know it would make a big difference in how you feel about yourself and how you interact with others. There are enough things in life we tend to worry about. Imagine how your life might change if you could free yourself from anxiety over the way you look.

My passion for writing this book is to help you achieve confidence in your image so that you'll have more time and energy to focus on what's most important in your life. Looking great certainly isn't everything, but it has a way of bringing out the best in us. So . . . let's bring out your best!

*B*ette DeHaven

Chapter
ONE

K

I remember standing in the grocery store and glancing over at a woman filling her cart. I couldn't help but stare. She either wanted to be stared at or had no clue about how she was presenting herself. She had a great figure, which I'm sure she worked hard at, but her designer jeans were so tight that I couldn't figure out how she could even walk in them. And her sweater was so low cut that one wrong move and . . . well, you can imagine—hello! I'm sure you get the picture. Her bleached blond hair was teased really high and the stiletto heels looked out of place in the produce section. To top it off, her dark brown lip liner looked like my 1st grader's outline in his coloring books and the rest of her make-up was no less severe.

7

Although it was certainly interesting, what fascinated me even more than looking at her was watching the men. Unlike the stares *you'd think* she would get, I watched two different men shake their heads with this, "What was she thinking?!" look. I couldn't help but feel the urge to make her over from scratch and show her how truly beautiful and dazzling she could look without the whole get up. With properly fitted clothes, a current hairstyle, and softer make-up, heads would have turned with a positive response.

I do, however, want to give her some credit here. She put a lot of effort into creating her image. So, maybe she went a little overboard but at the other end of the spectrum are those who put no effort or thought into how they look. Granted, it's very enticing to just throw on an old t-shirt, sweat pants or jeans with tennis shoes, and put your hair in a ponytail. But what's the message you're sending? You're probably hoping that your first impression says, "I usually don't look like this. I'm just really busy today." What it's really saying is, "I put no thought or consideration into how I present myself—I could care less!" How do you want others to perceive you? Do you want them to know that you care about yourself and others, or would you rather they perceive you as sloppy, uncaring, and disorganized.

Don't get me wrong. I'm not saying you can't look really great in a t-shirt and stylish jeans with your hair tied back, but if that's more your style then let's do it so people say, "Wow! You look awesome."

Whether our style is overdone or underdone, it all boils down to knowing what to do. It's just like a magnificent five course meal. None of us are born knowing how to put it together. If you're like me, you've blown it more times than you care to remember. Under cooked, over cooked, too much seasoning, not enough seasoning, it takes quite a few tries to get it just right. Our own personal image and style is no different. We're not born knowing how to put it all together successfully. Wouldn't it be great to be able to follow a simple recipe for personal style? Once you've used the recipe several times, you can alter it to your tastes and claim it as your own.

Despite how you may be feeling about your appearance today, or how you may have struggled with personal style in the past, *A Recipe for Your Best Personal Style* is the right solution to looking and feeling your very best. Our confidence comes from the changed lives of thousands of women who have learned and applied the principles in this book; principles based on the premise that you have a unique beauty and style all your own. We choose to focus on all that you are, not all that you aren't, and believe that enhancing the beauty you already possess is one of the significant steps to experiencing greater success in life.

Like the sage advice of our grandparents, you may not find anything shockingly new in this recipe, but you will glean from it the direction you seek. Your coloring, your personality, your body frame, and your likes and dislikes are the key ingredients to developing a truly fabulous style. Have you ever searched frantically for your glasses only to find out the obvious? They are sitting on top of your head. This recipe is so simple and obvious, yet overlooked by so many. Once you see it, you'll wonder why it never dawned on you before.

Grab a highlighter pen, cozy up in your favorite chair, and join us on this new venture to cooking up your best personal style. Just like that favorite family recipe, we promise the results will be unforgettable!

Recipe

There are no ugly women; there are only women who do not know how to look pretty.
~ Antoine P. Berryer

Chapter

TWO

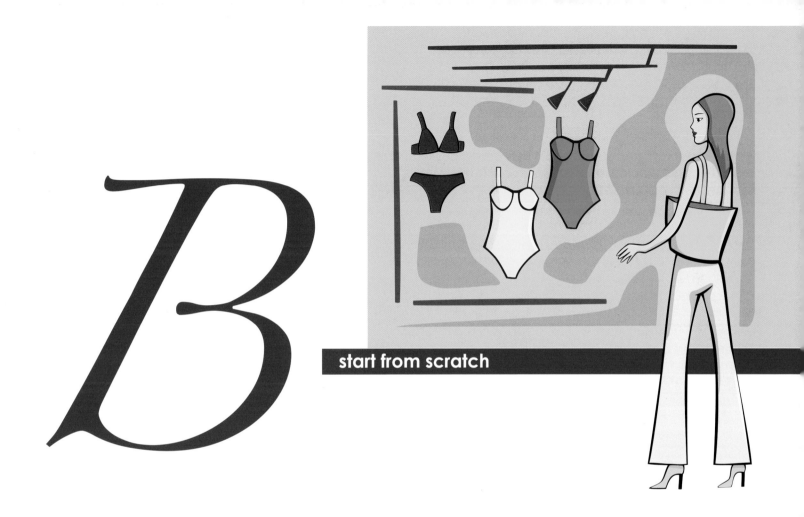

B

start from scratch

Don't you love it when springtime is in the air and flowers start blooming? The warm sun feels so great and the anticipation of a wonderful summer makes each day a little brighter. The coats and sweaters find their way to the back of the closet making room for bright, cheery sundresses and sandals. Maybe you're like me and try to get an early start on some summer shopping. The quickest way to ruin my day is to head to the department store in search of the perfect swimsuit! Don't you love standing in those dressing rooms with their three-way mirrors and fluorescent lights . . . Ugh! Who were those swimsuits designed for anyway? It's enough to make me wish it were winter again.

11

Most of us grew up with Barbie and at some point while we were dressing her in another one of her beautiful gowns, we looked at her legs, then ours, her bust, then ours, her waist, then ours and noticed a difference, didn't we? We knew she was the epitome of beauty . . . there was no question about that . . . so, what did that make us? And would Ken still love us if we didn't look like Barbie?

Tragic, but true—Barbie has left many of us feeling somewhat less than adequate in the figure department. Did you know that it's been estimated that if Barbie were 5'6" instead of 11 ½ inches tall, her measurements would be 39-21-33? It's been said that a woman's likelihood of being shaped like her was less than 1 in 100,000! In 30 years of working with thousands of women, I have yet to find even a handful that fit the Barbie doll body profile.

Now, it wouldn't be fair to blame all our insecurities on Barbie. Unfortunately, TV, movies, magazine covers, and advertisements serve as a constant reminder to our feelings of inadequacy in a society that has become obsessed with perfection. On any given day, almost *half* of the women in this country are on a diet and countless others are considering surgical procedures as an alternative. We are convinced that we don't measure up . . . but to what? An absurd standard has been set! The average American model stands 5'11" tall and weighs 117 pounds. In contrast, the average American woman is 5'4" tall and 140 pounds. Now come on. Why are we comparing ourselves to a handful of women who spend hours in "hair and make-up" before ever being photographed. Well, guess what, with special lighting and some air-brushing we could all look like super models!

Let's come to grips with the body we have. "Start from scratch!" When you start from scratch in making a recipe, you have the freedom to use the ingredients that best fit your needs and tastes. No pre-packaged or standard ingredients that someone else came up with. You can experiment by adding or deleting your own ingredients in order to come up with the best results. It's time to start from scratch and create your own recipe for style. Get rid of all the "pre-packaged ideas" that you should measure up to the model standard. I have heard it said, "Everyone needs to learn to love their body." I would be happy if we could just "make peace with it." We're always wanting something we don't have, aren't we? If we have curly hair, we want straight. If we have stick straight hair, we dream of curly waves. Sound familiar? If we're short, we want to be taller. If we're too tall, we want to be shorter.

Make "peace" with the body you have!

Have you ever noticed women who don't fit the model image but always seem to look great and have it all together? Even though they may be 30 lbs. overweight or stand only 5'2", they carry themselves with a sense of confidence, satisfaction, and pride. They walk to the beat of a different drum and have a different attitude about themselves. They are at peace with their body and they are beautiful!

Finding and wearing the right clothes has been my "Cinderella experience" to making peace with my body. I am a size 8 - 10 and people look at me and think I have no figure problems just because I am "petite." But bottom line, every woman dislikes certain parts of her body and for me it's my thick waist and flat rear-end. Growing up I could never wear some of the styles my friends wore that accented their waists and showed off their curves . . . since I didn't have any! Eventually, with some trial and error, I discovered how to create the *illusion* of that "perfect body" with clothes. In truth, good style has nothing to do with our weight. When our clothes fit correctly, our bodies look better. It's really that simple. But somewhere along the way, with each stage of life, whether in our teens, post-pregnancy, or when those hot flashes start, we get ourselves hung up on all of our figure problems. In reality, we have a *fit* problem not a figure problem. The key is that everything we don't like can be disguised or down played. My personal self image has greatly improved since those teen years because I have learned to "maximize the positive and minimize the negative."

Recipe

Learning to make peace with your body
is a process, not an event.

Challenge yourself to make peace with your body and begin to value what you see in the mirror. I know, I know. It's easier said than done. Cut yourself some slack. Remember, it's a process, not an event. Begin with baby steps and you'll be amazed by what can happen for you. Here's how!

Change your attitude.

Change your attitude about your body. Remember, you and I are the norm and normal women live everyday with imperfections. This little attitude adjustment will free you up to make better choices. I'm sure you don't give it a second thought when your car needs a tune up to run more smoothly, so why not give your attitude a check up when you look in the mirror? Get rid of the negative self talk and understand that there is not one of us, no matter how perfect our body appears, who does not dislike something about it.

Instead of seeing this . . .

See this!

We can flip through the pages of entertainment magazines and daydream all day, but even the best of celebrities have body part models that stand in to create the perfect body. According to a recent article I read, our endless pursuit of perfection has created a $160 billion-a-year global industry, encompassing make-up, skin and hair care, fragrances, cosmetic surgery, health clubs, and diet pills. And that doesn't even scratch the surface when you add in clothing, shoes, accessories, and all the other adornments. Stop chasing perfection and comparing yourself to an unrealistic standard.

Comparison is the cause of most of our unhappiness with our bodies.

I often reflect back to my twenties when I found the first sign of cellulite on the back of my legs. I remember how upset and depressed I felt. From then on, every time I thought about it or looked at my legs in the mirror, it was all I could focus on! Instead of being thankful that I didn't have more, I obsessed over it. Talk about needing an attitude adjustment. What I wouldn't give years later for just *one* little bump!

Stop making excuses—make a decision!

Once you change your attitude about yourself and stop making comparisons, it's time to take the next step. Stop waiting to be good to yourself and drop the excuses! Don't live in the "just as soon as" zone. "Just as soon as I lose these extra pounds . . . as soon as I get the promotion at work I can afford to . . . when the kids are in school" . . . If you wait for just the right time, it's never going to happen! Make the decision to be good to yourself now. Start applying the principles in this recipe and enjoy some results. You are worth it! Think of the possibilities!

Focus on what you CAN change not what you CAN'T!

You CAN'T change the proportion of your hips but you CAN down play them by wearing a solid color pant with a fun jacket or brightly colored top. You CAN learn to draw attention away from your "hated body parts." You CAN value what you have now by playing up your positive features. If it is your eyes and your hair, learn to make them look fabulous with great eye make-up and a flattering hairstyle. If you have nice legs, wear a great skirt and show them off. Once you start receiving compliments, you will begin to feel good—really good about yourself. Before you realize it, you'll focus less and less on what you can't change.

While I don't qualify as a world-renowned expert on self-esteem, I have worked with enough women to know one thing—we are much too hard on ourselves! Remember, we don't step out into the world each day the same way we step out of the shower . . . stark naked. Thank God! Since we cover ourselves with clothes, why not learn to do it in a way that creates a body we "feel good in"?

I work with a woman who has struggled all her life with a low self-esteem, which goes hand in hand with the fact that she has been overweight since the time she was in elementary school. She's our "behind the scenes" detail person. She's great at what she does but has spent her life hiding. She never wanted to get involved in anything, hated going to new places and meeting new people, never felt like she had anything much to offer, and rarely smiled. Recently, I made the comment to her that she gets more beautiful every time I see her. Her reply, "It's because I am finally learning to love who I am and making peace with my body." Twelve years ago when we met, those words would have never left her lips. She is still 35 pounds overweight and getting past a painful divorce.

So what's different? She has learned to value what she has and dresses her body beautifully. Feeling good in "her skin" has allowed her the freedom to meet new people and do things she never would have dreamed of doing. Not long ago, she stood on stage at a style show. She was confident and her smile was contagious! She has had her Cinderella experience, and *this* "Cinderella" is a size 14.

My desire is that as you read through this book it will inspire you to take action in whatever area you need to change. My personal journey in the area of self-image has been one of gradual acceptance. This is not about trying to look like someone we are not, but rather looking and being the best you and I can be.

Begin by putting all of your "baggage" behind you. Start from scratch with a new perspective. Think of yourself as the beautiful, unique, sexy woman you are and come on a journey with us to a better self-perception. Your future is waiting.

Chapter

THREE

R

color: the essential ingredient

Ever had one of those so-called "ugly days"? A day when your skin looks pale or blotchy, your hair looks dull, and everyone keeps asking if you feel okay. I can bet with confidence that part of the reason you didn't feel and look your best was because you weren't wearing the right color. I know it sounds a little far fetched but color is actually the first essential ingredient to personal style. It applies to your choices in every area of your image: hair, make-up, clothes, shoes, accessories, etc. Aside from its well-known ability to affect our moods and perceptions, color also has an interesting affect on our appearance. It can make us look younger or older, smaller or larger, alive or tired, clear or blotchy, balanced or off kilter. And just like if you use salt when the recipe calls for sugar, no matter how great the rest of the ingredients are, the wrong color can ruin the outcome.

I remember I was in my early 30s when I first heard about Color Analysis from my sister living in California. Nobody here in the Midwest really knew anything about it, but it was all the rage out there and she was so anxious to "do my colors." When she came home that summer for a family reunion, I must admit I was not that excited about it, but agreed to let her drape me. Once she completed the initial draping, she was thrilled to inform me that I was a "cool winter." She showed me some of *my* colors, like deep red, fuchsia, royal blue, purple, and charcoal gray. All I could say was, "What about khaki, olive, cream, brown . . . you know, all the colors I love to wear?" She told me I don't look good in those colors because they don't complement my skin tone. Instead, they made me look washed out. "So," I said, "give me a skin graft!" Needless to say I was not interested in being a "cool winter." The good news . . . she and her drapes went back to California and I continued to wear the colors I loved, oblivious to the reasons why I shouldn't.

That Christmas, my sister sent me a hot pink blouse as a gift. I remember writing the thank you note, but thinking in the back of my mind that I would never be caught dead in it. However, one dreary day at the end of January I was in a rut and getting sick of wearing the same old things over and over again. As I searched through my closet, desperate to find something I hadn't worn in a while, there it was—way in the back—that hot pink blouse with the tags still on it. In a moment of insanity, I decided to give it a try. In order to wear it, I had to change my regular make-up colors so I rummaged through my make-up drawer and found some pink blush and lip color that would work.

When I got to the office that morning and took my coat off, the attention I got in just 5 minutes made me feel like a million bucks! I was surprised by all the compliments about how great I looked, how my eyes sparkled, how thin my face looked, how pretty I was . . . I had always heard, "Ruth, I love your outfit!" but that day the compliments were about how *I* looked. I realized then that some colors we wear and some colors wear us! You would think that hot pink would be wearing me but the opposite was true. It was "my color." My hair, skin, and eyes were in balance with the color and the result was a flattering personal image. People noticed *me*, not my great blouse.

There are colors we wear . . .

and there are colors that wear us.

While the extreme popularity of color analysis has come and gone, knowing and wearing your best colors is one of the easiest things you can do to always look your best. When you wear the *right* colors, your eyes sparkle instead of looking tired, your skin appears smoother, and you look healthier, slimmer, and more youthful. When you wear the *wrong* colors, you get questions like, "Late night?" or "Don't you feel well today?" People may only notice your outfit and not YOU.

Some of us will gravitate to our best colors naturally. For the rest of us, we might as well be color-blind.

How do you determine your "right" colors?

Don't fall into the trap of letting your color choices be influenced by friends and family, the current fashion trends, or the ever-fluctuating hormones. When choosing your colors, you need to be objective and choose colors that mirror your natural coloring and create balance and harmony. There are two steps that will help you to determine your best colors.

STEP 1: Determine if you are WARM or COOL.

The first step is to realize that everyone can usually be classified WARM or COOL. Your skin and hair color are the factors that will help determine this. If you haven't seen your natural hair color in years, look at your roots or eyebrows for a hint. You can also think back to what your hair color was when you were a child. Pull out some of those old photos and reminisce.

Look in the mirror and compare your characteristics to the ones listed in each category and see where you fit.

If you are WARM, your *natural* hair color will be golden to strawberry blonde, honey or golden brown, chestnut to very dark brown, red to auburn, or yellowish gray. Your skin will be milky white or ivory, often freckled, peach, or golden. Your skin may have a thin or transparent appearance. Often your face and neck will flush very quickly and obviously. If you are a woman of color, your skin will be a *golden* brown.

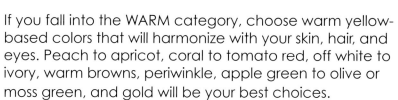

If you fall into the WARM category, choose warm yellow-based colors that will harmonize with your skin, hair, and eyes. Peach to apricot, coral to tomato red, off white to ivory, warm browns, periwinkle, apple green to olive or moss green, and gold will be your best choices.

If you are COOL, you will have little to no honey yellow, gold, or red in your hair, skin, and eyes. Your *natural* hair color will often have a cool smoky cast. It may be ash blonde to deep ash brown, dark brown, black, gray, or salt and pepper. Your skin may be china doll white, beige, pinky or rose beige, olive with a gray green cast, *cool* brown, or black.

If you fall into the COOL category, choose cool blue-based colors that will harmonize with your skin, hair, and eyes. Chalk white, powder blue to navy blue, powder pink to fuchsia to cherry red, pale gray to black, mint green to hunter green, and silver will best compliment you.

STEP 2: Determine what colors balance your hair, skin, and eyes.

After figuring out what category of colors is best for you, determine what depth of colors will create balance and harmony with your natural coloring.

It's actually a pretty simple rule of thumb. The darker your hair, skin, and eyes are, the *darker*, *richer*, and *brighter* your colors can be. The lighter your hair, skin, and eyes are, the *lighter* and *softer* your colors will need to be for balance and harmony with your natural coloring.

Dark Cool

Light Warm

Light Cool

Dark Warm

If you are still confused on cool or warm, the following questionnaire may be helpful.

Your Best Colors Questionnaire

Choose only one answer for each question. There is no correct or incorrect answer. If in doubt, go with the first answer that comes to you. Follow your instincts, not what someone suggested or told you to wear or choose.

1. Refer to the two color groups shown. Circle the group that contains most of the colors you naturally prefer to wear.

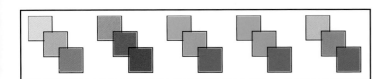 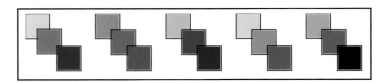

2. Circle the shade of red you feel best wearing.

■ Medium pink (c)		■ Blue red (c)
■ Warm peach (w)		■ Chili red (w)

3. Circle the blue you feel best wearing.

■ Medium blue (c)		■ Royal blue (c)
■ Bright aqua (w)		■ Deep turquoise (w)

4. Circle the yellow you feel best wearing.

□ Light yellow (c)		□ Lemon yellow (c)
■ Bright warm daffodil (w)		■ Mustard yellow (w)

5. Check off which jewelry colors you would choose if wearing only a watch and a ring or two?

___ Matte silver, antiqued silver, pewter, white gold, fresh water pearls, emeralds, or rubies (c)
___ Silver or white gold, black onyx, and bright clear gemstones like rich amethyst (c)
___ Fine gold, yellow gold, opals, coral stone, cream-colored pearls, and topaz (w)
___ Rich gold and shiny copper, bronze metals as well as antiqued gold, amber, tiger-eye, jade, and orange coral (w)

6. Check off what type of complexion you have. Hint—look at the inside of your forearm.

___ Cool blue undertone (c)
___ Olive or gray green undertone (c)
___ Blue pink undertone (c)
___ Black with blue undertone (c)
___ Black with warm undertone (w)
___ Golden, peach, or creamy yellow undertone (w)

7. Are your freckles (not age spots) . . . ?

___ Non-existent (c)
___ Brown (c)
___ Golden brown (w)

8. Is your hair color (before adding any color or highlight) . . . ?

___ Black (c)
___ Medium brown (c)
___ White blonde (c)
___ Golden brown (w)
___ Chestnut (w)
___ Silver gray (c)
___ Creamy gray (looks highlighted) (w)

___ Blue black (c)
___ Light brown (c)
___ Ash blonde (smoky)(c)
___ Auburn (w)
___ Copper (metallic red) (w)
___ White (c)

___ Dark brown (c)
___ Ash brown (smoky)(c)
___ Golden blonde (w)
___ Red (w)
___ Salt and pepper (c)
___ Golden gray (dull) (w)

Answer Key

Add up your answers.

\# of (c) = Cool _____

\# of (w) = Warm _____

If you have a greater number of cool answers, it is likely that you are cool. If you have a greater number of warm answers, you are most likely warm. The main indicators of whether you are cool or warm are your skin, hair, and eye color. Please use this questionnaire as a secondary indicator.

Although these things give you some basic direction for choosing the right colors to wear, you may also want to seek advice from a trained color consultant. They will be able to provide you with more specific color choices and a color fan to guide your buying decisions.

Having a clear direction for your clothing, accessories, make-up, and hair color choices is certainly a huge benefit. But if you're like I was, you're thinking that most of your closet is full of the wrong colors and you can't afford to go buy all new clothes. Don't think you have to trash your whole wardrobe. Even though you may have many things that aren't your best color, the change can be gradual.

Begin by looking at the items you have in your closet and see what you can work with right now. Focus on putting your best colors by your face with a top or accessory to offset the "not so good colors." I had a beautiful and expensive tan pantsuit that I had just purchased and I was NOT getting rid of it. Instead, I purchased a purple top to wear with the outfit. Not only did that top work as a transition piece, it also had the versatility to work with any future purchases I would make because it was one of my colors.

The one thing you don't want to do is spend any more money on unflattering colors. Purchasing the *wrong* color of shoes or top in order to wear something in your closet is not a good decision. Every time you buy something new, make sure it is a flattering color on you.

It takes about 2-4 years to completely make the change to a "color friendly" wardrobe. This may seem like a long time, but your life will begin to simplify immediately. Once you know your best colors, you can instantly eliminate certain selections. As you shop, you'll spend less time searching around for things. If you stay consistent, eventually everything in your closet will harmonize and complement each other allowing for greater simplicity in your closet and in life. Say "goodbye" to costly mistakes that waste your money and closet space and say "hello" to the compliments you're going to receive. You're going to love getting dressed every day!

Low Fat Color

Want to instantly look like you lost 10 pounds? Do it with color...

● Wear one color head to toe to look taller and thinner.
● Match your top to your pants or skirt color with a different color jacket to create a vertical, slimming line of color.
● Wear dark to medium colors with no shine.
● Avoid wearing light or bright colors on areas of your body you want to minimize like hips, rear-end, or large bust.

Chapter

FOUR

R

toss it up!

Is it time to make a change?

Do you ever look back through old photo albums and laugh at the crazy styles of clothes you wore over the years that you wouldn't be caught dead in now? Styles change and we change with them. So, what about your hair in those photos? Have you kept the same style or a slightly different version of it year after year? Why is it that we have long since gotten rid of those old clothes, but we keep wearing the same hairstyle? For some of us, our hair is like a security blanket. It's safe . . . It's comfortable . . . It's familiar . . and it's a part of who we are. But it may also be the "final frontier" to looking our very best.

I am a perfect example of someone who was unwilling to change my hair. For over 30 years, I wore my long hair, pulled back smooth, braided in a ponytail, and wrapped against the base of my head. It was impossible to have a bad hair day. It took me less than 5 minutes to do and it was so easy I could have done it in my sleep. Why change what's working, right?

This signature hairstyle of mine became a part of me in my early 20s when Aqua Net hairspray was about the only option for hair care products. Hair cutting techniques were also limited at that time and since I had medium thick, baby fine hair that was hard to create a style with, much less hold one all day, it was natural for me to do what was comfortable. And like so many things, it became a habit. Well, time sure did pass and the rest of the female population tried new looks and new products while I still sat on the edge of my bed, without a mirror, fixing my hair. Before I knew it, I was over 50 and in desperate need of a change.

Although I was in denial about it, my hairstyle was aging me before my time. Something had to change. And since a new mini skirt, fish net hose, and a body hugging sweater was out of the question, I contemplated changing my hair. The thought of my security blanket being cut up into a million little pieces scared me to death.

"What if it looks silly?" "What if I can't do it by myself everyday?" "What if it takes me too much time to style it?" A million thoughts of resistance reeled through my mind. But in the end, my desire for change outweighed my fears and I took the plunge. Wow, did I ever receive compliments! I looked and felt stylish, years younger, and just plain great! Looking back, I couldn't help but wonder, "What took me so long?"

Do you agonize over decisions to cut your hair, color it, or change the style? And after making a change, do you find yourself going right back to styling it the same old way? A lot of our identity is wrapped up in our hair so we often stay with what feels comfortable. Unfortunately, what's comfortable tends to lead us to a style that is too long, outdated, or even just no style at all. If change were easy, we would all do it . . . and much sooner! But please, do as I say, not as I did.

Be open to new ideas and different looks with your hairstyle.

We can have it all together nose to toes—wearing our best colors, the perfect outfit, great shoes, and flawless make-up—but without a great hair style to "top off" the look, we appear unfinished and unmindful of the "total package." A great current hairstyle, on the other hand, adds credibility, polish, and pizzazz to our over all image.

If you're ready to "toss it up" and make a change, the following tips and suggestions will help.

1. **Find a talented hairstylist.**
   - Solicit recommendations from friends and family.
   - "Shop the streets"—when you see someone with a great cut/style, pay them a compliment and ask who does their hair.
   - Look for three important things—someone who keeps current but not too trendy, is experienced with your hair type, and is easy to communicate with.
   - Keep in mind you may have to try 3 or 4 stylists until you find one who is right for you.

2.   Schedule a consultation.

- Allow extra time when you book your appointment to discuss your options with your hairstylist.
- Talk about what you want, the amount of time you can spend on your hair, and your styling abilities (or lack of) in order to get the best style recommendations.
- Look at photos and agree on a hairstyle that—goes with your lifestyle, is age-appropriate, fits your body, complements your facial features, and is suited for your hair type.

3.   Get a great cut and maintain it!

- Go with a hairstyle you know you *can* and *will* duplicate at home.
- Schedule regular appointments to maintain your cut (about every 6 weeks).
- Shorter hair will need to be trimmed more often.
- Don't forget to "toss it up" every now and then by changing your style to avoid getting in a rut.

Once you find a stylist, get a consultation, and follow through with a great cut, there's no stopping you! Except for . . . a recipe gone wrong! We can ALL relate to that. Where we usually make our mistakes is with chemical treatments and styling.

Recipe gone wrong!

If you color your hair, don't stray too far from the original recipe. Subtle highlights are always safer and more flattering than extreme changes. Do your homework on store brands if you're a "do it yourself" kind of gal. Be prepared to pay more for color application in a salon. Make sure you come home feeling great. And never accept a color that is bad or has damaged your hair.

35

When considering other chemical treatments, remember that the best hairstyle for you is one that suits your natural hair type. Straightening and perming your hair to make it do something it doesn't naturally do can often result in damaged, split ends. So, unless your hair is exceptionally healthy, stick to using other methods to tame curls and add volume. Choosing the right cut, products, and tools designed for your hair type will give you the results you want to achieve.

Speaking of results, have you ever come home from the salon feeling great about your new hairstyle only to have it disappear the next day after washing it? Well, you're not alone. Many of us have trouble duplicating and maintaining a healthy new hairstyle at home, but the good news is there's a "recipe" to remedy that!

1. While it's a great time for relaxing, instead of taking a "cat nap" while you get your hair done, pay attention to the products, tools, and techniques your stylist uses. A good stylist will take the time to show you how to style your hair. Then, practice at home.

2. For the best styling performance, know what products to use and how to apply them.

- Use products specifically formulated for your hair type.
- Rinse your hair well before applying shampoo to help eliminate product buildup.
- More is not better. Using too much product weighs down your hair.
- Comb through hair after applying a styling spray, cream, gel, or mousse to cover all your strands.

3. Keep your hair healthy for great results every time you style it.

- Get rid of split ends and dead weight—trim long hair regularly.
- Prevent damage to hair—avoid using hot water and high heat settings on hair dryers.
- Increase the strength and growth rate of your hair—limit intake of caffeine, carbonated drinks, and complex carbs.
- Get plenty of rest, drink lots of water, eat a healthy diet, and ask your doctor to recommend supplements you may be lacking.

A good hair day is a good day. A bad hair day is a bad day. Unfortunately, there are far too many bad hair days walking the streets! Don't be one of them.

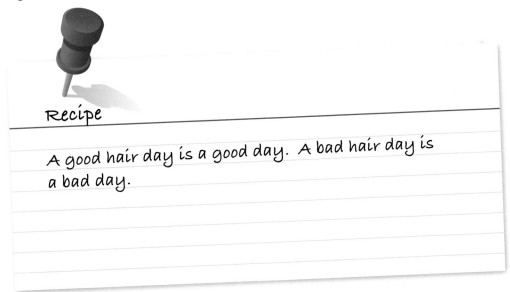

Recipe

A good hair day is a good day. A bad hair day is a bad day.

Chapter
FIVE

Ahh...the fountain of youth. You know when a wrinkle and a pimple show up on the same day, it's down hill from there.

Have you ever tried to take a short cut in a recipe and skip some of the "prep time" like letting the dough rise completely or marinating your meat overnight? It doesn't ever quite come out the same does it? Every recipe calls for a little prep time and this one is no exception. I like to think of using good skin care as my way of preparing my skin for make-up but it's also preparation for younger, healthier looking skin. What you do to your skin *now* will show up in the years to come.

Why does the appearance of our skin matter? Can't we just cover it up with make-up? Well, we could. But rather than settling for a damaged canvas to apply our make-up to, why not improve the canvas? With the advancements in science and technology, we now know that aside from genetics, there are things we can do that make a difference in the look and feel of our skin.

Many women's magazines which used to focus on make-up now give equal attention to articles and ads on skin care products and how to have healthy looking skin. Why? Because we are learning that good skin is the result of a regular skin care routine along with a healthy diet, exercise, drinking plenty of water, and getting a good night's sleep. That's a tall order for most of us, given our busy lifestyles. Not only are we neglecting to do the right things for our skin, but we continue to damage it by doing things we may or may not know are harmful. Smoking and excess alcohol can wreak havoc on our skin and sun exposure is just plain BAD! Even going to bed with make-up on clogs our pores and causes breakouts.

The good news is we CAN have younger, healthier looking skin. The bad news is we do have to work at it! For many of us, having good skin will require a lifestyle change and a commitment to begin taking care of our skin inside and out. Although there are many things we can do to get the maximum results, even changing one thing to start with will make a difference (like wearing sunscreen). So, examine your daily routine, your budget, and your goals, and then decide what you are able to commit to doing.

Remember... Whatever your age may be; it is never too late to start taking care of your skin. A daily skin care routine, good nutrition, and a few daily disciplines will help you to achieve younger, healthier looking skin.

Daily Skin Care Routine

Skin care helps preserve youth and we certainly all want that! Daily skin care should begin at puberty. The key is to use your skin care twice a day, every day, seven days a week. Will there be days you miss out of sheer exhaustion? Of course. But, strive to make it a priority in your day.

Skin care doesn't have to be an "event." Try incorporating it into the time you're already spending doing other things. You can throw your face cleanser in the shower and wash your face then. Apply your toner and moisturize your face, in a matter of moments, before you do your hair or while you're deciding what to wear. Bottom line, we always seem to find a way to make time for what is important in our life, don't we? Aren't you important? Isn't taking care of you a priority?

Finding the time for skin care should definitely be a priority *at night*. Did you know that every night you go to bed with make-up on, you are aging your face at least 5 days? I have found that if I know I am in for the night, I sneak away early in the evening and take 10 minutes for my skin care. That way I don't wait until the end of the night and wind up falling into bed too tired to take care of my skin. I have a friend who puts her cleanser on her pillow every day to remind her not to go to bed, no matter how tired she is, without her skin care. Find a trick that works for you and make using your skin care a daily routine.

What products should you use for your skin? With so many different products out there, it can be confusing to know where to start. In this section, we'll talk about the basic products that you should strive to use, and we'll also discuss the extras you may want to consider based upon your personal needs and the time you are willing to invest.

Recipe

Nature gives you the face you have at twenty; it is up to you to merit the face you have at fifty.

~ Coco Chanel

Start with a Basic Skin Care System:

Not all skin is created equal. There are skin care systems formulated specifically for varying skin types. These include: oily, combination, dry, sensitive, and acne prone. Choose a three-step system for your personal skin type that includes a *cleanser*, *toner*, and *moisturizer*.

Why use three steps? Why not just soap and water? Well, the cleanser is specifically formulated to cleanse your face without drying it out or causing a wax buildup that soap leaves. Not using a toner is like putting your clothes in the wash and skipping the rinse cycle. And, even if you have oily skin, it needs the hydration from a moisturizer, which also helps protect your skin from the environment.

Who doesn't LOVE special treatment?

There are so many wonderful special treatment products out there. Technology has brought us a long way from the "miracle" products we tried even 5 years ago that didn't work. Many of these new products have *proven* to offer great results! Here are a few you might like to try.

Eye Creams
When you walk by the mirror smiling and do a double take noticing the crow's feet in the corners of your eyes . . . it's time! For me it was around the age of 25, about the same time that first gray hair literally popped up. Eye creams are made especially for the delicate skin around the eyes to treat and protect. They are great for reducing the bags and dark circles under our eyes as well as those fine lines.

Sun Damage Repair
Did you know there are products that will help repair sun damage? Many lotions are available that will minimize the wrinkles caused by sun exposure. There are also skin brighteners to help improve skin tone and lighten brown spots due to sun damage.

Blemish Treatment

Why is it "they" always pop up just days before that big event? No matter your age, you know what I'm talking about. The dreaded zit! Well, we no longer have to hide out waiting for it to just go away. Try a blemish treatment that will heal and treat breakouts without damaging your skin. For more serious acne there are skin care systems formulated to help control breakouts.

Facial Scrub

We wonder why men seem to age more "gracefully" than we do. Well there's a reason for that. Most of them do something to their face everyday that we don't. They shave! The cells in the top layer of our skin are replaced every 45-74 days. Exfoliating regularly to slough off the dead surface cells allows for new cells to create a younger healthier complexion.

Many of the cleansers on the market double as a scrub. But for some of us, exfoliating every day is too much for our skin. If that is true for you but you still like the thought of having just one step, then you can buy them separately, and on the days you want to use a scrub, simply mix the two together in the palm of your hand for a one-step wash and scrub. Use your scrub at least twice a week. Be sure not to use a body scrub on your face. Find a *gentle* one specifically for the face.

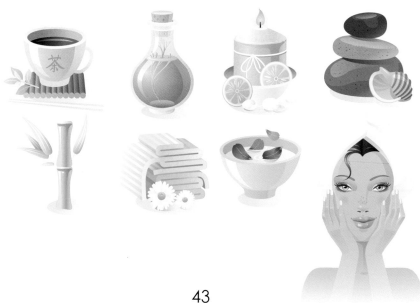

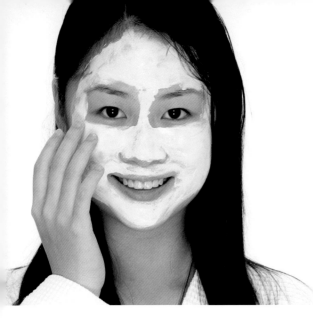

Facial Mask

Imagine. The candles are lit, you're relaxing in a hot bubble bath, your favorite mask tightening on your face, and listening to the beautiful sound of soft music when reality hits. "Let go of my Ipod!" "Get out of my room!" "Honey, have you seen my Sports Illustrated?" "Uh...who gave the dog those M&M's?" In a perfect world, masking while soaking in a bubble bath works, but in my world, I pamper my skin while multi-tasking. It's a discipline I find time for while I'm paying bills, writing a thank you note, making breakfast, or in the shower shaving my legs.

Choose a mask formulated for your needs, whether it's dryness or oily skin with clogged pores. Fit it into your schedule 2-3 times a week if possible. Hey, just because we don't have time exclusively for skin care doesn't mean our skin has to look like it!

Anti-Aging Products

We, as consumers, spend billions on skin care products alone! And those sales are motivated by our desire to turn back the hands of time and defy the signs of aging. Over the last decade, there have been tremendous strides in skin care technology allowing us to achieve more youthful skin. This has all become possible through increased knowledge in the prevention of free radical damage, enabling a delay in the onset of wrinkles and, in some cases, even repairing sun damage. Halleluiah! It's a proven fact that many of these anti-aging products really do work. Do your homework and find out which ones can make a difference for you.

One last thing about skin care. Follow usage instructions on the packaging and seek a trained skin care consultant if you want to expand your knowledge on choosing the right products for you.

Let's not forget those hands and feet!

Give your hands and feet the royal treatment. Treat yourself to that occasional professional manicure or pedicure. If your budget doesn't allow for this luxury, pamper your hands and feet at home.

- Simply keep your nails neat, clean, and unstained.
- Keep nails filed at an even length.
- Buff nails to a shine or wear a clear coat of polish.
- If you enjoy colored nail polish, great! Just be committed to keeping it up.

Good Nutrition

Beautiful skin is a result of good nutrition.

Yesterday I had such a busy day. Well, all last week was busy. Come to think of it, where did last year go? I found myself running to the post office, on to a meeting with a client, to the market, etc...etc... Before I knew it, my stomach was growling at me and I realized I hadn't stopped to eat all day. So... you know how it goes. I drove through a fast food restaurant for a burger, fries, and diet coke combo meal minus the "recommended daily allowance" of vitamins and minerals. I know I am not alone. So often we choose convenience foods that are void of any nutritional value because we haven't got the time to prepare three square meals a day. And when we do have time to eat healthier meals, it isn't always as healthy as we think it is. The things we get at the market nowadays lack the proper amounts of nutrients due to the way foods are processed, transported, and stored for profit, not nutritional value.

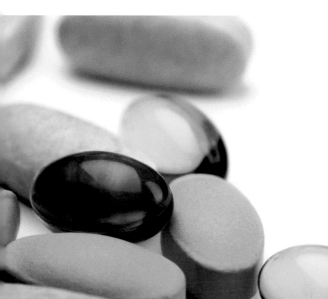

According to Dr. James Meschino, "No matter how good a moisturizing cream is, you can never achieve the level of soft, smooth skin that you have the potential to attain unless you provide your body with optimal doses of essential fats and specific vitamins and minerals through nutritional supplementation."

Supplementing your diet with vitamins and minerals is a smart choice in order to have and maintain healthy, youthful skin. We recommend that you do some research and talk to a few experts to determine what supplements and herbs will be right for you.

Daily Disciplines

Recipe

It's never too late to start taking care of your skin.

Let's take a look at some of the controllable factors affecting our skin and what we can do to take better care of it. With discipline comes reward. Without it, we face consequence.

1. Avoid Smoking

Smoking will age you! If it were as simple as all things in moderation, we wouldn't have to discuss it. Unfortunately, as with many other things in our lives, few people can smoke in moderation. Bottom line, smoking is harmful to your skin because it deprives your skin, the largest living organ in your body, of oxygen. It destroys your healthy coloring and causes crow's feet and lines around the mouth as well as other signs of premature aging.

2. Limit Your Alcohol Consumption

Have you ever noticed someone who has a lot of tiny red lines or veins showing on their face? These are usually more prominent on and around the nose and cheeks. Broken capillaries in the face can be caused by consuming an excessive amount of alcohol.

3. Get Plenty of Sleep

Oh yes, that's easy enough. Tell that to the college student "cramming" for exams, or the new mom waking up every two hours for feeding time, or the executive who needs that report done by 8am the next day. Though we all have times when we don't get a good night's sleep, just remember that a lack of sleep will show up on your face and, over time, age you. So be good to yourself and get some ZZZZZ's.

4. Exercise

If you aren't already on the move, check with your doctor first and get moving. Busy, stressful, and sedentary lifestyles can cause skin challenges like acne and rosacea. Walking 20-30 minutes a day is a good start to reduce stress and get your blood pumping.

5. Drink More Water

If you drink your quota of water every day, CONGRATULATIONS! You've "tapped" into one of the easiest ways to contribute to healthy, beautiful skin. Did you know our skin is mostly made up of water? On average, we need 64 to 72 ounces of water a day to maintain good hydration and healthy skin.

6. Always Wear Sunscreen with UVA and UVB Protection

Wrinkles are primarily the result of sun exposure and heredity. Sunscreen is not only your protection against skin cancer, but it is also the best weapon against UVA induced wrinkles. Make sure you wear it everyday. Some moisturizers and foundations have SPF in them now to make it convenient.

Though we will never again have the smooth flawless skin we had as children, it doesn't matter how old we are, it is never too late to start taking care of our skin. Any little bit of "prep time" will definitely affect the outcome of the recipe. Make your skin a priority. Decide today to follow the principles of *daily skin care, good nutrition,* and *daily disciplines.* See for yourself how wonderful your skin will feel—not to mention how great your make-up is going to look. When your girl friends start giving you compliments and asking for your secrets, you'll know the changes you made were worth it! And the results will motivate you to keep going!

Recipe

If I had known I was going to live this long,
I would've taken better care of myself.

~ Eubie Blake at the age of 100

Chapter
SIX

the frosting on the cake

Birthdays, weddings, baby showers, and graduations are all special occasions where, no doubt, cake will be served. Whether it's simple or elaborate, the "frosting on the cake" is the part of the recipe that definitely enhances the taste, gives it that finished touch, and sends the message.

Ask just about any man and he will tell you that you look just fine without make-up. What he's probably really saying is that he doesn't want to wait on you while you primp. Like the frosting on a cake, make-up enhances the natural beauty of every woman. It also creates a finished look and can definitely make a statement. Why settle for "just fine"? If you've been playing with make-up since you were old enough to reach your mom's dresser and enjoy trying out the latest and greatest looks, go for it! If on the other hand, you were the girl slinging a ball bat alongside the boys, I can bet that for you applying make-up is a chore. You need to find that one great, but easy look you can rely on.

51

Make-up is an art not a science!

Whether creating a "super cool" race car birthday cake, some fun cupcakes for the 4th of July, or that elegant "one of kind" wedding cake, putting that "frosting on the cake" is definitely an art not a science. It takes one's own personal style, the right tools, and *practice*! Applying make-up is no different.

No matter what look you are going for, or what your personal style or preference may be, understanding make-up products and how they should be applied is the key to creating the look you want to achieve. However, like fashion, make-up is constantly changing and evolving to reflect the latest in trends and technological advances. From celebrities who continually change their look, to cosmetic companies trying to stay on top, there are many factors influencing what the hottest new looks are. And isn't it so true, that when we see something that looks good on someone else, we want it too?

How's a girl supposed to keep her make-up bag up-to-date in the ever changing world of cosmetics? Well, with make-up, mom's advice that, "Just because everyone else is doing it doesn't necessarily mean we have to," certainly rings true. Stay focused. Start with the basics—your *make-up bag essentials*. Then, depending on your style and the look you are going for, explore new products and techniques to stay current. Who knows. You may follow the trends and even totally reinvent your look from time to time, but you will always rely on your basic products and techniques.

When applying make-up:

- Always start with a clean face.
- Choose colors that harmonize with your hair, skin, and eyes.
- Invest in a good set of brushes and sponges.
- Apply make-up in good lighting.
- BLEND, BLEND, BLEND

Make-up Tools

Brushes and Sponges

The right tools are a must and a make-up bag essential. Don't rely on your fingers or the brushes that come with the make-up you purchase. Keep your brushes handy.

Basic wedge make-up sponges—use for applying foundation, blending concealer, and fixing little mistakes. Wash your sponges often.

Small angle brush—use this brush for lining the eye with shadow, coloring the brow, or applying concealer.

Large and small dome eye shadow brushes—use in place of the sponge applicators you get in the package to create a light, dusty, more natural application of product.

Cotton swabs—use to blend eyeliner and clean up small mistakes.

Blush brush—use this dome shaped, medium size brush to apply blush for a natural look vs. the cheek stripes you get by using the small narrow blush brush that comes in the package.

Powder brush—use this large dome shaped brush to distribute powder evenly and lightly.

Let's take a look at the products and techniques for Preparing the Canvas. Your *concealer*, *foundation*, and *powder* work together to create a smooth, even, flawless skin surface, which acts as the canvas for applying the rest of your make-up.

Concealer

Even if you prefer a minimal make-up look, a concealer is one product you won't want to be without. It's a make-up bag essential! Concealer can help hide dark under-eye circles, blemishes, scars, birthmarks, rosacea, expression lines, etc. It also acts as a foundation for the eyelids.

A stick concealer will be adequate coverage for most of your needs. However, for bigger scars, birthmarks, or to cover rosacea, a creamy concealer applied over your foundation usually works best. The color of your concealer should closely match the color of your skin or be slightly lighter in color.

Application Tips:
- Apply with fingers or for best results use a small angle brush.
- To blend, dab with a sponge.
- Apply to: eyelids, corners of mouth, lips, smile lines, inside eye corners, and under eyebrow arch or any area you want to "lift" or conceal.

Recipe

For flawless make-up . . .

SKIN CARE FIRST!

Foundation

We would all agree that choosing a foundation is the most frustrating part of make-up application. Finding just the right color, consistency, and coverage in a foundation is the key to a smooth and natural looking application. Fortunately, most cosmetics companies have now categorized their foundations for easier selection so you can choose one for your color range, skin type, and coverage preference.

Choose a color that closely matches your skin tone. The best way to do this is to apply a few shades in small stripes along your jaw line to find the one that blends in or "disappears" on your skin.

Next, choose the formula that is best for your skin type (dry, oily, or sensitive) and decide what coverage you want: sheer, medium, or maximum.

Foundations are not a "one type fits all" product. Look at foundations that you can "try on" before you buy. See how it looks on your skin in natural daylight. Apply the foundation and wear it for a day before making a decision. Take the time and effort to find the foundation that is just right for you. You'll be glad you did!

Application Tips:
- Apply foundation with a sponge for best results.
- If it's skin, (including eyelids and lips) you cover it with concealer or foundation.
- Use long strokes from center of face and blend outwards.
- Use upward strokes to apply on forehead.
- Blend well along jaw line.
- The more lines you have in your face, the less foundation and powder you should use.

Powder

This is another make-up bag essential.

Powder sets your foundation and keeps it from "disappearing." It also creates a smooth, matte finish for the application of your blushes and eye shadows. A loose translucent powder is your best choice, especially if you have oily or combination skin. It contains no oil so it does the best job of absorbing and controlling your oil and shine. A pressed powder is a good option to carry with you for touch ups.

Application Tips:
- Apply with a large fluffy powder brush.
- To avoid uneven distribution, shake off excess powder from brush.
- After applying foundation and concealer, dust powder over entire face including eyelids and lips.
- If you like a bronzing powder, apply with a large blush brush to areas naturally "kissed" by the sun.

Blush

This is your next make-up bag essential. A lot of women don't use blush, but think about the benefit. It's a quick step and a great way to give your skin a healthy glow. Be sure to coordinate your blush color with your skin tone and clothing. Choose a pink or rose red blush if your skin tone is cool. And for warm skin tones, choose a peachy pink to apricot shade. Your goal with blush is a natural glow. Avoid shades that are too dark, too bright, or too brown for your coloring.

Brush on the color.

Application Tips:
- A good powder blush glides on quickly and easily with a quality blush brush.
- Always tap off excess blush from brush and apply to cheeks with a light touch.
- Using an upward circular motion, starting directly beneath the center of the eye and no lower than the bottom of your nose, sweep blush along the base of the cheekbone moving toward the hairline.
- Blend and soften edges of blush with a sponge or brush over with loose powder for a natural look.

Eyebrows

Your eyebrows are a great indicator of your moods and feelings. They can express surprise, sadness, anger, frustration, and even happiness. Eyebrows also express and reflect the current fashion. They have gone from pencil thin to Brooke Shields "full" and back to thin again.

Whatever the trend, your eyebrows are an important feature. They are the frame for your entire face. Many women don't realize what an amazing difference grooming their brows will make for their image. Eyebrows that are well groomed will open up your eyes and give you a fresh, finished look. Oh... and one more benefit, they can make you look younger!! If you have never touched a tweezers to your brows, take one last look in the mirror and say good-bye to those unruly brows.

Shape up your brows!

To "shape up" your brows, you have a few different options. They include waxing, threading, or tweezing. A quick side note—you never want to shave your brows since this will create an undesirable 5 o'clock shadow. Waxing and threading are typically done professionally in salons. These procedures are relatively painless. Ok . . . so it totally hurts, but it only lasts a moment and the results are worth it! The benefit with this method is that you can rely on a professional to shape your brows if you aren't comfortable doing it yourself. Once you have them professionally shaped, you can maintain them by tweezing at home.

If you decide to shape your brows yourself at home, your best option would be tweezing. You could wax them but it removes a larger area of hair at one time and you may end up with unfavorable results. Follow the tweezing tips and shaping instructions below for beautiful brows.

Tweezing Tips:
- Use a 5x magnified mirror in *good lighting*. Natural daylight works great!
- Tweeze brows after a hot shower or hold a warm wet washcloth to brows before tweezing to open the hair follicle and make the process less painful.
- Tweeze only one hair at a time.
- Tweeze hairs out in the direction of hair growth.
- Take your time.

Recipe

Low, thick brows that close in the eyes look masculine and age the face.

Shaping Instructions:

- The best rule of thumb is to follow the natural shape of your brow and simply define it by tweezing stray hairs.
- The beginning of your brow should be in line with the inside corner of your eye. Hold a pencil or brush handle vertically along side your nose and line up the inside edge of each brow with the inside corner of each eye. Remove hairs outside that line.
- The arch of your brow should be above the outside edge of your iris and the outside portion of the brow from the arch should slant slightly downward.
- The end of your brow should fall just beyond the length of your eye. Hold a pencil at an angle from the bottom of your nose along the outside corner of your eye to find where your brow should end.
- Don't over do it! Start with tweezing less if you are unsure about which hairs stay and which go.
- Maintain your new brow shape by tweezing the new hair growth about once a week.

Some eyebrows may be too sparse in places. Define and fill them in where necessary with an eyebrow pencil or try brushing on a little eye shadow using a color close to your natural brow color. If using a pencil, rather than drawing one thick line, use short strokes to resemble natural hairs.

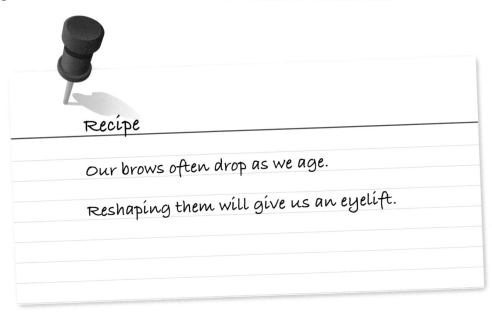

Recipe

Our brows often drop as we age.

Reshaping them will give us an eyelift.

Eye shadow

Depending on the results you want, and the time you have to spend, there are a multitude of options in eye shadow colors and application techniques from which you can choose. It can be fun to copy the fashion magazines and use the latest and greatest eye colors available to achieve that promised look: sexy, fun, innocent, or classic. However, eye shadow is the most challenging of all the make-up products to apply. So . . . practice makes perfect. And remember, using a good set of brushes to apply your shadow will make all the difference.

Whatever your comfort level may be, start with a basic look that works for your eyes and then "express yourself" by learning new techniques or fashion trends. Look to the make-up artist at your hair salon or a consultant in your area for help in achieving the right look for your shape eyes and style. If you prefer a more natural, low maintenance make-up look, then simply applying concealer and powder to your lids or a light neutral shadow from lash to brow will do the trick.

Using a good set of cosmetic brushes will make eye shadow much easier to apply.

Application Tips:
- Be sure to prep the eyelid for shadow with concealer, foundation, and powder.
- A matte finish is best for all ages.
- Choose colors within your cool/warm color range or stick to neutrals.
- Large dome eye shadow brushes are best for applying your all over color and for blending.
- Use small dome eye shadow brushes for applying contour color.
- Angle brushes are for lining and accenting the eye with shadow.
- Use a light color shadow from lashes to brow.
- Use a medium to dark color to create a contour in the crease of your eye.

Eyeliner

Although eyeliner is not always essential, and many women will choose not to wear it everyday, it can be a great way to define and enlarge your eyes. When eyeliner is applied below the eye, it enlarges it. When it is applied above the eye, it enhances the lashes. For the best look, apply eyeliner both above and below your eyes, but avoid closing the lines to the inside corners of your eyes.

Application Tips:
- A pencil liner will be the easiest to use.
- Draw the line close to your lashes from the outside corner of your eye toward your nose. Blend with a cotton swab or blending brush.
- To set your liner to last longer, brush over the lines with a small angle brush using a similar neutral shadow color.

Mascara

Mascara is another make-up bag essential. Even for a minimal make-up look, it's a quick and easy way to finish the eye and fill in those lashes that are not thick and black naturally. Choose a shade according to the lightness or darkness of your overall coloring.

Application Tips:
- You may want to curl lashes for best results before applying mascara.
- Mascara is a great product, but if you don't want to lose your lashes, be sure to *completely* remove your mascara every night!

Lipliner

Lining the lips is essential to a great lip line and good color application. Remember when you colored pictures in a coloring book as a child? Didn't you find it easier to outline the picture first and then fill it in with color? Well, it's no different with your lips! Lipliner helps prevent lip color from bleeding into the fine lines that are inevitable as we age. It also gives your lips a smoother, more youthful look and enables you to create those pouty, sexy lips by slightly extending your lower lip line at the bottom. Select a lipliner color that is similar to your lip color.

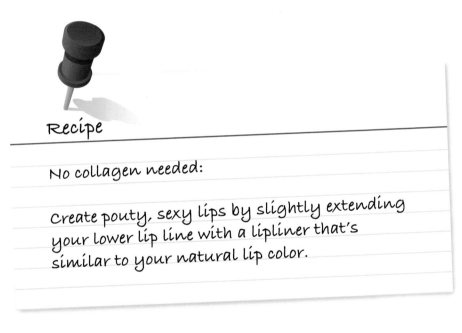

Recipe

No collagen needed:

Create pouty, sexy lips by slightly extending your lower lip line with a lipliner that's similar to your natural lip color.

Application Tips:
- If you are satisfied with your lip shape, follow your natural lip line.
- Start lining the center of your top lip by creating a V. Connect the top of the V to the corner of your mouth on each side.
- To line your bottom lip, start in the center with a small straight line and connect to the corners of our mouth.
- Fill in the rest of your lip with the pencil for longer lasting color.

Lip Color

Lip color is a make-up bag essential but it doesn't mean you have to wear lipstick! From lip gloss, to lip stain, to tinted lip balm, your lip color can come in a variety of forms. Find one that suits your style. Choose a cool or warm shade that complements your skin tone or goes with a neutral shade for a natural look. Keep in mind that frosted shades magnify the lines in your lips. Choose a creamy color or colored gloss for the appearance of younger lips.

Application Tips:
- For longer lasting color, apply lipstick with a lip brush.
- Make sure your color choices balance with the depth or lightness of your hair and eye color. If they don't, you will either be "all lips" or look washed out as though you forgot your lip color.

Finish your make-up look with a great smile. Consider teeth whitening if needed. There are over the counter products that work great and are inexpensive. Your smile is one of the most important features in making a positive first impression, so don't hide it!

Recipe

Rememeber that a smile will always make you more approachable.

There are very few women who do not benefit from wearing make-up. Why not start trying out some of the basic tips shared here? Don't forget the products that should be your make-up bag essentials: brushes, concealer, powder, blush, mascara, and lip color. Practice the techniques and don't be afraid to experiment with new products you haven't used before. It may take a few tries before you find the right colors and become comfortable in your application, so give yourself permission to fail. Before long, you'll be a pro at using make-up to enhance your unique beauty and create the look you desire. Remember, this recipe for make-up application is an art, not a science. Have fun and enjoy putting the "frosting on the cake!"

Smile. It counts!

Chapter

SEVEN

R

the secret ingredient

Are you ready for a Cinderella experience?

When I find the perfect fitting pair of jeans for my figure, I feel like I won the lottery. Life is good! Know what I mean? The quest for clothes that fit our bodies and flatter our figures can be so frustrating. It's often a game of hit or miss and trying on every thing in the store is exhausting. What's the secret to finding clothes that fit and flatter?

We've all oooohed and aaaahed over talk show makeovers or the before and after photos in magazines where a woman's figure is transformed simply by changing a few clothing items. Surely, it must be trick photography, right? No, it's the real thing. How'd they do that? A closer look at a frustrated gal wearing a fitted top tucked in to her high-waist blue jeans reveals large hips, a small bust, and narrow shoulders. A few hours later she emerges like Cinderella, happy and confident with her new look. A flattering pair of dark jeans minimizes her hips, a colorful jacket adds width to her shoulders, and a great fitting bra gives her boobs a lift. I often wonder, "When the fairy tale dust settles and she goes home with her one great outfit, what happens then?" She can't take her personal shopper home in her hip pocket. She's left with one fabulous look and confusion as to how to duplicate it.

It reminds me of my great grandmother's homemade apple pie. It was always a big hit at every family gathering. I have attempted many times to make her recipe but it never quite turns out the same. Something is missing. It almost seems like when she passed on the recipe she left out one secret ingredient making it impossible for anyone else to duplicate granny's pie. It doesn't surprise me though. She always was a feisty little woman.

Like granny's pie, knowing the secret ingredient for dressing our bodies makes our *Recipe For Your Best Personal Style* a big hit not only with others but also with us!

Shopping for women is the most rewarding part of what I do. It's like giving someone that Cinderella experience—a complete vision of who they can be and the freedom to wear styles they never dreamed they could wear! I can't tell you how many times I find a number of outfits for a client in the same store where she walked in and said, "I can't find a thing!" My clients often say they "get hooked" on wanting my shopping service. That's great for my ego but I would really like to work myself out of a job. I would love for my clients to know how to make great clothing choices so I am not needed. I want them to be able to confidently walk into a store and consistently duplicate the looks that I have pulled together for them. I want to pass on the recipe with the secret ingredient. Dressing the body successfully is about creating optical illusions and focusing on fit. That's it! *That's* the big secret.

Creating Optical Illusions

You probably have at least a couple of outfits that look great on you and always seem to bring on the compliments. What is it about those outfits that you find so flattering? Without even realizing it, you have applied the secret of creating an optical illusion. Whether small, average, or large, we all have a few figure challenges we are looking to disguise. It may be a short neck, big hips, small bust, or protruding tummy. Whatever it is, we all know what body part is our biggest frustration.

Optical illusions are about using *clothing lines and details*, *good proportion*, and a *proper fit* to disguise the parts of our bodies we feel concerned about while at the same time highlighting our assets. The result is the illusion of a balanced or well-proportioned body. No matter what your body shape and size, finding clothes that fit and flatter will be simple once you know what to look for in your clothes.

You can disguise a major figure challenge and no one will ever notice unless you mention it.

Start by looking at the shape, color, and details of your clothing choices. These are the things that will either be your friend or your enemy. If your body proportion is small from waist up but large from waist down or vise versa, learn what you can do with your clothing choices to minimize the larger area and maximize the smaller area to create balance. Think of it this way. To minimize the acid taste in a tomato based dish I usually add a couple teaspoons of sugar to balance out the taste. This is a trick I learned from my mom and it works great.

Vertical and Horizontal Lines

To balance out the body, one of the best tricks is the use of vertical and horizontal lines to create optical illusions.

Vertical lines minimize, disguise, elongate, and draw attention away from figure challenges. They create the illusion of a slimmer figure by drawing the eye inward and upward. They are good for disguising any heavy or thick parts of the body such as a short neck or wide hips as well as a full bust and thick arms.

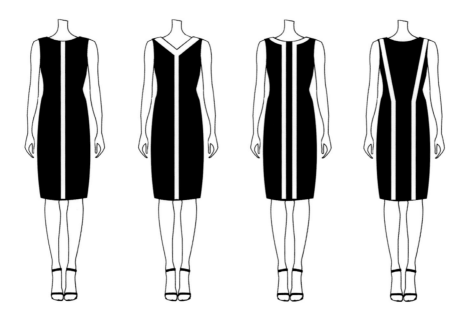

Vertical lines can be created by more than just a stripe of color. Dress in monochromatic (one) color from head to toe to draw the eye up and down rather than across. Rows of buttons, v-necks, and even creases in a pant leg can create a vertical line. Watch out for vertical lines that are spaced far apart on clothing. They can add width by drawing the eye out across the body and we certainly don't need that.

Say, for instance, that you are very fit and trim but your figure challenge is a short neck and narrow shoulders. Turtlenecks are not your friend. Your best neckline is a v-neck opening which will create a vertical line.

Horizontal lines enlarge and add width to narrow parts of the body. But beware, they can add width to your wide areas, too. They will draw the eye out on the body creating the illusion of width for sloped or narrow shoulders, and enhance a small bust or a flat butt. Avoid horizontal lines on broad shoulders, a full bust, and large hips.

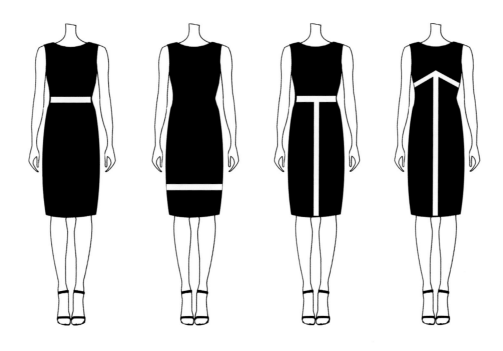

Horizontal lines are often created with contrasting colors, belts, cuffs, and pocket flaps. A square neckline will draw the eye out on the body making narrow shoulders appear wider. Your hemline, whether on a skirt or sleeve, can also create a horizontal line so be careful where it hits. For example, short sleeves add width to a heavy arm so choose long sleeves or ¾ length instead. Also, be aware of wrinkles and creases that will create horizontal lines, especially across the hip area on pants and skirts.

Color and Proportion

Another way to create optical illusions to balance the body is with color and proportion.

- Dark colors minimize—light colors maximize.
- Bright colors attract attention—so wear them where you want the eye to focus!
- Wearing all one color or monochromatic dressing creates a slimming effect. It does not need to be black or a dark color.
- Proportions of things like, the size of a print, details such as buttons, and your accessories: jewelry, shoes, handbags, etc., will affect the appearance of the weight and size of your body.
- Keep in mind that when small items surround (or are placed on) the body it appears larger and large items make the body appear smaller.

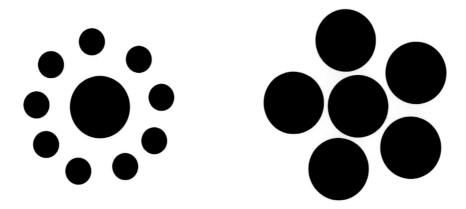

Although the center circles are the same size, the one with the smaller circles surrounding it appears larger. The same principle of proportion applies to our body frame.

Use shapes, colors, and details in your clothing to create the illusion of a balanced body.

Fabrics, Details, and Accessories

The fabrics, details, and accessories you choose can also help you to create the illusion of a balanced body if you learn what affect they have and how to use it to your benefit.

- Bulky fabrics will give an impression of added weight.
- Wear bulky clothes on the thinner part of your body.
- Shiny fabrics reflect light and cause the body to look heavier. Matte, textured fabrics absorb light and flatter a large figure.
- Fabrics should hang well on your figure without clinging.
- Pleats, pockets, and lapels are details that will add width or draw attention so consider where they are on the outfit and how they will affect your look.
- A belt worn on a thick waist only draws attention to it but wear the belt inside of a jacket and instantly you have the illusion of a smaller waist.
- A medium to high heel shoe can add length to your legs for a slimming look.
- Consider your hairstyle a detail or accessory that will work in your favor. A fuller style can balance a larger figure but overwhelm a petite figure, especially if it is too long. You can even disguise a long neck or rounded back with the right hairstyle.

Now that we know the different ways clothing lines, details, fabrics, and proportions will affect the look of our bodies and have some basic tips for creating the illusion of balance, let's talk about getting dressed! Since it is impossible to have a list of every item of clothing you should or should not buy based on your body shape, the key is to look at a each piece and evaluate what it does for you or "to you." What lines are being created? Evaluate the color, pattern, and fabric texture. Then decide if it is right for you based on your fit challenges.

The following are some examples to help guide you:

Full Bust

DON'T

- Wear horizontal stripes on top—they maximize an already full bust.
- Wear tight fitting tops—they hug the full bust, as well as any other midriff bulges you may have, making you look larger.
- Wear patch pockets on shirts—they draw attention to the bust and add bulk where you don't want it.
- Wear rolled up sleeves that stop at crest of breast—this look creates a horizontal line drawing the eye outward and enlarging the full bust.
- Wear wide belts—they shorten the torso and make the bust appear fuller.
- Wear details on your top that draw attention to your bust line.

DO

- Wear v-necks to create a slimming angular line.
- Choose small lapels or none at all to avoid added bulk or drawing attention to the bust.
- Choose solid colors and medium weight, matte finish fabrics. Shiny fabrics and prints, as well as heavy fabrics, will add bulk and the illusion of width.

Heavy Arms

DON'T

- Wear clingy fabrics or tight fitting sleeves—they hug the arm and make it appear bigger.
- Wear very short sleeves—they expose the arm by putting a line at the fullest part and drawing attention there.

DO

- Compensate for full arms by wearing a looser fitting sleeve made of a more structured fabric.
- Wear ¾ length or full-length sleeves.

Wide Hips

DON'T

- Wear bulky fabrics—they add width.
- Wear pants or skirts too tight—they hug your shape and make you appear larger. Clothes should fit tastefully loose on the body. If a skirt or pant waist is too big, have it altered.
- Wear tops that end at your hips creating a line that adds width unless it's the same color as your skirt or pant.
- Wear pleats—they add width especially if they don't lay flat.
- Wear horizontal lines or pockets on hips—they draw attention to your figure challenge and create width and bulk where you don't want it.

DO

- Put the details of your outfit above the waist to draw the eye upward, away from your problem area.
- Wear smooth fabrics in solid or subdued vertical patterns.

Based on the principles of creating optical illusion, consider the following questions when making your clothing choices:

- What is my figure challenge? What are my assets?
- How does line, color, fabrics, and proportion help me maximize the positive and minimize the negative?
- What am I looking for in an outfit?
- What do I want to avoid?

If you stand up straight, you'll look thinner and your clothes will hang better.

Focus on Fit

Recipe

You know it's a bad day when you put your bra on backwards and it fits better.

~Anonymous

Whether you are "well endowed" or don't think you have enough there to bother with, a good fitting bra will make all the difference in how your clothes fit.

A few years ago I had a new client who was vice president of a Fortune 500 company. On top of being a successful businesswoman, she was busy at home as a wife and mother of two, the youngest of which was only ten months old. As you can imagine, she had very little time to focus on herself. She hired me to help her create a professional look for work. After an initial visit to her closet to help determine how I would create a great new look for her, we set a time to meet at the store of her choice. Being as busy as she was, she had only 45 minutes to devote to our shopping trip so I arrived early and prepared a dressing room for her with ten outfits she could try on.

Michelle was about 5'4", 35 lbs over weight, a size D cup, but nicely proportioned. As she began trying on the outfits I had selected for her, she mentioned to me that, though she was no longer nursing, she was still wearing one of her nursing bras. Being the frugal woman that she was, she figured she might as well wear them out.

As she continued to try the outfits on one by one, it seemed everything she tried made her look frumpy or matronly. Now, I've always taken great pride in my ability to analyze a woman's style and size based on her body proportions, comfort level with clothes, etc., and I was sure that I had pegged Michelle to the tee, but after the 7th outfit, I began wondering if I had lost my touch. Nothing seemed to be working.

All of a sudden, it hit me. I knew what was wrong—it was her bra! I don't just teach, I preach about the importance of a good fit in a bra, yet I had completely overlooked the obvious. We were running out of time so I had Michelle get dressed and took her to the lingerie department to have her professionally fitted for a bra. Well, the end of the story is a happy one. Michelle bought 8 of the 10 outfits we originally rejected and she went home looking and feeling like a million bucks.

When it comes to getting dressed, being in the right fit and style of bra not only increases comfort, but also helps our clothes to fit better and look great. Finding the right bra isn't just about being fitted in the right size. We all have different needs in the shape, style, and amount of support. When was the last time you were professionally fitted for a bra? If your answer is "Never," or "Over a year ago," then head over to a department store in your area and ask someone in the lingerie department to fit you properly.

Once you have discovered how great you look and feel in your clothes with the right bra, there are a few things you should consider in order to maintain that great look. Because bra styles constantly improve, be sure to get fitted at least once a year and take advantage of new options.

You will also need to replace your bras every 3 to 6 months depending on how often you wear them. A worn out bra will offer less support and change how your clothes fit. If you are full busted or sagging as you age, you will definitely want to invest more in the bras you buy. This will help to ensure you get the support and shaping that you need.

Even if you think investing in a bra is a waste of money, don't make any hasty judgments until you've seen the difference for yourself. A poor fit in a bra does not flatter our figure or make clothes fit better. We wouldn't think of making macaroni and cheese without real cheese would we? Okay, maybe we would. I admit that box of "mac and cheese" satisfies a hungry brood and is quick and easy but . . . it doesn't look and taste as great as the real thing!

A poor fit in a bra does NOT flatter our figure.

Keep it under wraps!

Let's discuss undergarments in a little more detail. First of all, wear them! Secondly, use good taste in your choice of undergarments and how much skin you reveal. You don't want anyone you meet thinking, "That's way more information than I wanted to know about you." Keep in mind what message you may be sending. I am sure that some of us aren't even aware of what we may look like from behind or how much we reveal when we move around.

Here are a few Undergarment Do's and Don'ts:

- DON'T let thong panty bands show above your pants or skirts, and never show your crack!

Recipe

Wearing the correct undergarments will make your clothes fit and look better.

- DON'T allow bra or panty lines to show through your clothes. This can happen when clothes are too tight, a fabric is too thin or see through, or when undergarments are too tight. If this is a problem for you, make sure you are wearing the correct size undergarments so that they are not cutting into you.

- DO wear a shaper/control undergarment or structured fabric, if necessary, to create a clean line, eliminate the appearance of cellulite, and avoid jiggle in the rear. Regardless of your budget, there are many good choices available.

- DON'T wear thin or see through blouses and tops with a sheer bra.

- DO wear a strapless or matching color bra with tank tops or other revealing tops.

Always remember. It's about Fit not Size!

With the right fitting bra, you will now be able to have a flattering fit in your clothing choices. Let's talk about size. As women, we are often guilty of a preoccupation with size. Tell me you haven't done it . . . walking into the dressing rooms, your arms loaded with clothes to try on, that look of hope in your eyes, and then half an hour later coming out empty handed with that look of disappointment and disgust. And what do we do next? We go home and have a pity party with a pint of ice cream or a bag of cookies!

Why is it we go to pieces over a *number* on a tag? If we are ever going to find the right clothes, the first thing we need to come to grips with, is the fact that the number on the tag is irrelevant. One brand size 14 fits like a size 10 in another brand. It's because our clothing is produced globally and sizing standards change. Depending upon the manufacturer, the model, and the standard that is used when designing clothes, sizes will vary dramatically from one company to the next. So let's focus on FIT not on SIZE.

Are you shopping in the right department?

Over the years, I have found three consistencies among women who look their very best:

- They don't care about size, only fit, because they know what it takes to look great.
- They are comfortable with their style.
- They shop in the right department.

Shop in the correct department to get the best fit.

Realize that it can take four different sizes in your closet to get a good fit. By the way, those are sizes that fit you now, not there for when you lose or gain weight. If you have challenges finding the right fit, you may be shopping in the wrong department. All things are not created equal, so here are some things to consider when determining where to find your size.

Height:
- 5'4" and under is Petite
- 5'5" to 5'7" is Average
- 5'8" and up is Tall

There are four main departments to shop:

Juniors—for teens and young adults. Junior sized clothes will be cut much slimmer over all to fit a less curvy figure. The styles will reflect a very young, trendy look. The junior departments are also carrying sizes now that cater to the plus size young girl with styles that reflect her age and cater to her clothing tastes.

Misses—is geared to fit the average height woman with sizes usually ranging from 4 to 16 or small to x-large. You will find a wide range of styles to choose from. Some manufacturer's pants and jeans will be sized in short, average, or tall lengths within this department.

Petites—will give you options from size 2 to14 and sometimes 16. If you're Petite, there are some significant benefits to shopping the Petite department. For example—compared to a size 10 in the misses department, a size 10 petite will have:

- Narrower shoulders
- Shorter rise in pant
- Shorter hem and sleeve lengths
- Smaller leg, arm, and neck openings
- Smaller details: lapels, pockets, and zippers

Women's/Plus Sizes—will offer sizes from a 14w or 16w and up. As with petites, a 14w or 16w will not be cut the same as a 14 or 16 in the misses department, or a 14 in the petite department. Compared to a department store, women's specialty stores will have even more size options and a greater style selection. This department often includes petite sizes for the woman who falls into the 16w and up size range but is 5'4" or under and needs the shorter hems, shorter sleeves, and shorter rise in pants.

Catalog shopping is a great option as well.

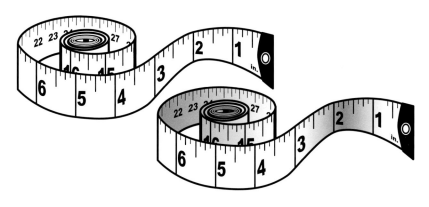

Over 50% of all women should wear a plus size on some part of their body. So, many of us will need to be shopping in two different departments in order to find the best fit. For example, my client Jenny who is 5'8" and wears a size 16w pant finds her best options in the women's department. But, since she is also a B cup with a narrow shoulder line, she wears a size 12 in tops and jackets, which she finds in the misses department.

If you have been frustrated in your attempts to find just the right size and fit for your body, don't throw your arms up in the air and just give up! Shopping is a learned skill; it takes time and a lot of trying things on to discover which stores offer the fit, style, and pricing that you are looking for. That's why it's called "shopping" not "buying." So rather than just running out when you need something, take a couple of trips for the sole purpose of learning. That way, when you do need something, you'll know exactly where to find it.

Consider alterations for a perfect fit.

Recipe

Men buy clothes and have them fitted, but women buy clothes and try to fit into them.

What if, instead of only wearing 20% of what you have in your closet, you were to wear 80% of it? Imagine that! Why is it that our closets are so full of things we just don't wear? In search of an answer to this phenomenon, I've asked many women why they gravitate back to the same few items in their closets time and time again. The answer always comes back something like this; "I like the color, it feels good on, it fits, it's comfortable, and it looks good on me. I get lots of compliments on it." Isn't it interesting that most of those answers have to do with having a good fit?

When you don't wear an item frequently, it is typically because there is something wrong with how you feel in it. You may try it again once or twice but it ends up back on the hanger taking up space in your closet!

Don't know where to find alterations? If you have a dry cleaner in your community, they will most likely be able to provide the basic alterations: hemlines, sleeve lengths, etc. Additionally, some department stores will offer a complimentary service to hem the items you purchase at their store so make sure to ask. If you try someone and are not happy, don't settle. Just keep looking. It is certainly worth having a good fit!

You'll feel great in your clothes when you have the right fit.

Good Fit Tips

How do you know if it's a good fit? Well, you'll know when you put it on and forget about it. You're not fixing, adjusting, pulling, and haggling with it or consciously thinking about how it looks on you.

Shoulders

Shoulders are actually the first place to start if you want to get a good fit. I have said for years . . . "Treat your shoulder line with respect and pay attention to how an item hangs on your shoulders." Before you put on a jacket, look in a mirror to see if you have obvious sloped shoulders. Maybe it's just one that is sloped. You'll know which one if your bra strap keeps sliding down on that side.

Fix sloped shoulders to have your clothing fit properly. Try a small foam shoulder pad that will balance your natural frame. Choose pieces with a more squared shoulder line and structured fabrics such as denim. Rounded shoulder styles and knits will only accentuate sloped shoulders.

Jackets
Your jacket collar should lie smoothly across the back of your neck. Any style jacket that can be worn open should have enough room to allow for a sweater or blouse when buttoned. There should not be any pulling across the shoulders or hips if buttoned or zipped. You should be able to reach forward without restraint.

Blouses or Tops
Traditional long sleeve blouses or tops should end at your wrist bone when your arms are hanging at the side of your body. Button front blouses must lie flat when you move your arms. No peek-a-boobs please! Wear nothing too tight or too short. Buy a larger size if you have to keep pulling your top down to cover skin.

Skirts
Skirts should have no creases or pull lines across the front at your hip line. Straight skirts should fall straight down in back and not cup under your butt. Hemlines should hang evenly from front to back unless designed to be uneven. You should be able to fit two fingers between the waistband and your body comfortably. If you can't move your skirt around front to back and vice-versa, the skirt is too tight. When wearing a straight skirt, no panty lines or cellulite should be visible.

Pants
Zippers and closures must lie flat with no pulling across your hips. Pant legs should hang straight from your hips and butt with no cupping or clinging. If the waist is too big but fits everywhere else, then have the waist altered. As with the fit of a skirt, so it is with pants. No panty lines or cellulite should be seen!

When you have the *secret ingredient,* the meal is sure to impress! Take the tips and tricks from this chapter and make dressing your body a successful experience.

Chapter
EIGHT

what's your flavor?

Recently, I searched my favorite online recipe site for a basic pancake recipe. My grandkids stayed with me for the weekend and we were out of pancake mix so I thought I could try them from scratch using just the basic ingredients like we "did in the old days." What I found in my search was two pages of every flavor pancake you can imagine. I was amused and also intrigued. Actually, it makes total sense. Pancakes to suit every taste. Why not? We are a society that is used to choosing from numerous flavors of ice-cream and almost as many gourmet coffee blends. Regardless of the choices of flavors, most of us tend to have our favorites that suit our tastes when it comes to coffee or pancakes or any other food. But haven't you been tempted to stray from your favorites to try something else because it was the special of the day, or someone recommended an awesome recipe you HAD to try? We need many different options available to us in food as well as all the other things we buy because we are not all alike. However, it means making choices. And sometimes those choices can be difficult because of so much variety in clothing styles.

Are there five different people living in your closet? And each their own "flavor"? At one time or another we have all purchased clothes on emotion and impulse or "emergency" rather than with the knowledge of what really expresses our personality and lifestyle. When you choose clothing and accessories to dress your body, you are expressing your unique, personal style and this style will affect everything from your clothing to make-up, hairstyle, and accessories.

I have a friend who prefers very casual style clothes. She owns only one skirt. Her daily "uniform" is blue jeans, a knit top, and a pair of athletic shoes. She prefers a simple, no fuss, hairstyle and very little make-up, if any at all. This dear friend is like good 'ole comfort food. You can always count on her. Her style is more traditional, practical, and comfortable like that great basic pancake recipe.

I, on the other hand, prefer outfits made up of coordinated pieces with accessories that tie in with colors I'm wearing. I only wear tennis shoes when I walk the treadmill! Although I enjoy convertible cars as much as the next gal, you won't see me in one going more than 10 miles per hour. My hair and make-up need to be done for me to be in my comfort zone. I guess you could say I follow a recipe to the T and I would be the whole grain, banana nut flavored pancakes . . . my husband would totally agree on the "nut" part. They may be a little more effort but totally worth it.

Then there is my sister. She wants to always wear the latest trends. When she walks in the room, it's like biting into your very favorite dessert. WOW! You always look forward to what's next. She watches fashion closely for the latest and greatest in clothing, shoes, and make-up. She is not afraid to be the "first" and hopes to be the only one wearing the newest style to an event. Her wardrobe is always changing because every season has new trends. And as you may have guessed, she's the chocolate chip flavored pancakes—which make no sense at all for breakfast—topped with a beautiful extravagant pile of whipped cream. But that is who she is and anything else wouldn't be right!

Great style is a result of *consistently* expressing who you are while feeling totally confident with the image you present. Many times we allow past influences to dictate our style. We can also get caught up in impulse buying or allow size and weight issues, or fashion trends to get us off track from expressing our true "personal style."

Has anyone ever said to you "That outfit looks just like you," or "This handbag is so you"? When a style "is you" it expresses your inner personality and makes you feel comfortable with yourself in any situation. Remember what Shakespeare said. "To thine own self be true." What styles make you feel confident but secure and satisfied? What styles do you put on that allow you to forget about yourself and just "do life"?

We tell the world who we are by what we wear.

It's time to take control over your wardrobe so that you can look and feel your best everyday. It will require some organizing and an evaluation of your personality and lifestyle but in the end the benefits will be awesome. Think about it . . . shopping trips made simple, an organized closet where you no longer try on 10 things before you find something that "feels good", and the ability to effortlessly create a great look everyday that exudes confidence.

Personal style is the fun part of this recipe. It's the next step that will give you specific direction in your clothing choices, accessories, hairstyle, and make-up look. Many of you may already have an idea of what your style is while others of you may still be searching. Remember, many factors affect what styles you have been choosing up until now. Put aside past influences and start from scratch.

Here are *three basic categories* for you to consider. Find the characteristics that best describe your lifestyle, preferences, and approach to dressing. You will most likely find the majority of your characteristics in one category with a few in the other two.

The Practical Casual

Your priority—Comfort

Some or all of the following may apply:

- You prefer casual clothes to dress-up.
- You are most likely a non-shopper.
- Your look must be easy to achieve.
- You rarely change styles and are satisfied with status quo.
- You often do not notice a need for change.
- Your styles must be safe and quiet; lacking in pretense.
- You like minimal make-up.
- You tend to wear a similar, no fuss, hairstyle year after year.
- You will buy several of the same style tops and bottoms.

The 40+ Casual—lives in jeans, t-shirts, sweaters and athletic shoes, boots or sandals - except when forced to dress up.

The 25-40 Casual—likes her casual comfort but also likes to be current with fashion.

The under 25 Casual—tends to wear what her peer group is wearing.

As a Practical Casual, you may be relaxed and easy-going or high energy and always on the go. You prefer a simple, practical, comfortable approach to everything you do including getting dressed. You are totally in your element when it comes to casual dress but dressing for business or special occasions just makes you want to stay home.

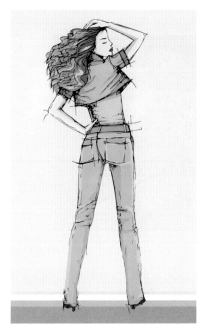  

The following will help you express your style and look great!

Make-Up
Though you prefer minimal or no make-up, a little make-up will go a long way to boosting your self-image and enhancing your natural beauty.

For casual everyday make-up wear: powder/foundation, mascara, and lip color or lip gloss. Add blush, one eye shadow color, and eyeliner for business and special occasions.

Hairstyle

Your preference will most likely be a loose or tousled style that requires minimal skills, time, and products. You may be prone to having no style at all to avoid the hassle. A great cut that is specific to your hair type and texture is the key to spending less time and effort to achieve a style. Many times a shorter cut will be the most flattering and easy to maintain.

In order to keep your style current, if your hair length is above the shoulders make sure your hair appointments are scheduled 4 to 6 weeks apart. For a successful business look, hair that is shoulder length or longer should be worn back in a smooth secure style.

Clothing Choices

Jeans, pants (when in style—capris, cargo pants, shorts), casual t-shirts, simple knit tops, sweatshirts, turtlenecks, khakis, cardigans, cable knit sweaters, unstructured jackets, cotton shirts, straight or A-line skirts.

Wearing solids will be your preference and the patterns you choose will be subtle plaids, stripes, or simple designs. Avoid clothing with shiny surfaces as they will cheapen your style.

Some tailored structure will be important at times to keep from looking too casual. You will rarely button your jacket even in business. You prefer clean simple lines—which means you will avoid flared hemlines, fussy sleeves and collars, and extreme necklines.

When shopping, choose separates that you can mix and match. This will give you the most freedom to express your style.

When it comes to accessories, you like to keep it simple. A nice pair of earrings that will go with everything, one good leather shoe will meet most of your needs, and one basic handbag that suits every occasion. On the other hand, don't be afraid to try more accessories.

Look for stores and designers that cater to your style: Coldwater Creek®, Eddie Bauer®, Talbots®, Cabela's®, Land's End®, Monterey Bay®, Liz Claiborne®, Ralph Lauren®, Banana Republic®, Abercrombie and Fitch®.

Once you know what you're looking for, you can duplicate your style by shopping the name brands and stores in your area.

For Business
- Keep it simple and easy.
- Focus on a great core piece, a modern pant or skirt; add a semi-fitted contrasting jacket with a conservative blouse or top, and a good pair of leather dress shoes.

Special Occasions
- A knee length straight or softly flared skirt will often work well. Pair it with a sweater set, a more open shoe with a slight heel, earrings, and maybe a bracelet.
- Another option could be a dress with clean simple lines.
- Lace or sequins are not necessary to be dressy.

Wardrobe tips / Do's and Don'ts
- Strive for good looking as well as comfortable outfits.
- Always wear a jacket for business.
- Don't wear clothes beyond their prime.

As a Practical Casual, don't allow your quest for comfort to keep you in the same uniform day after day. Make an effort to choose casual looks that will give some variety to your wardrobe.

Pay particular attention to your hairstyle. Keep it current and maintained, even if it is long! Get your haircuts scheduled 2 to 3 months in advance so your style is not grown out and lost before you realize it.

Recipe

When a style "is you" it expresses your inner personality and makes you feel comfortable in any situation.

Take the time to at least do minimal make-up for work or going out and about. It takes less than 3 to 4 minutes to dust your face with powder, apply mascara, a sweep of some blush, and lip gloss. Keep finger nails trimmed and buffed or freshly polished with at least a clear coat of polish. These disciplines will reward you with compliments that make you feel good about yourself.

Some of our most loyal and caring friends are Practical Casuals. You can count on her no matter what. When her dinner table is set, you may find mix and match tableware and maybe even plastic and paper goods. What the heck, it's not the way the meal is presented, it's spending time with family and friends that is most important to her.

A visible example in the media is Rachel Ray of "30 Minute Meals" and "The Rachel Ray Show."

The Modern Conservative

Your Priority—Fashionable with No Extremes

Some or all of the following may apply:

- You would readily hire a fashion advisor.
- You want to look current.
- You enjoy shopping but it's not your hobby.
- You want a current hairstyle.
- You always wear make-up whether casual or professional.
- You tire of your wardrobe and are ready for change.
- You are willing to make changes.
- You enjoy receiving compliments on your attire.

Spin-offs of the Modern Conservative:

The Elegant (refined, classic, luxurious, poised)

The Feminine (ladylike, delicate, dainty, demure)

As a Modern Conservative you are not a *trendsetter*, but definitely a *trend follower*. You enjoy making a statement. You appreciate compliments on your choice of style. You may, or may not, be comfortable choosing your look so you will seek advice.

Make-Up

You prefer a finished look and will take the time and effort to achieve it. Typically, your casual and business make-up will be the same. Your make-up application will include: foundation, concealer, powder, blush, eye shadow, eyeliner, mascara, lip liner, and lip color. If you are looking for a simpler look, follow the practical casual everyday make-up routine.

Hairstyle

A current but not trendy hairstyle is your preference. Whatever the style is, it will have an element of softness and control. It is important to you to take the time to style your hair everyday before going out in public.

Recipe

What's your flavor?

Practical Casual, Modern Conservative, or Risk Taker

Clothing Choices

Stylized jeans, capris, dress pants, shell tops, embellished knit tops, tighter weave sweaters, coordinated active wear, structured jackets, blouses, skirts, closed button suits, and dresses.

Many of the fabrics you wear are light to medium weight, rarely coarse and textured. Your fabrics will usually have a smooth look and feel. Fabrics that wrinkle, like linen, are not good for your style.

You will work best in solids or two color combinations. The patterns you should choose include florals, stripes, polka dots, or geometric prints.

You express your style best by buying coordinated tops and bottoms. You are an ensemble dresser—you like the look put together and worn the same way each time. You will not mix and match as often as the Practical Casual.

You express your style by always being finished with accessories. You will follow the trends and have the latest styles in shoes, handbags, hosiery, and jewelry. Often, you will put on heels with pants or jeans instead of flats or tennis shoes.

Look for these stores and designers that cater to your style: Anne Taylor Loft®, Bloomingdales®, Spiegel®, and most department stores. Designers such as Dana Buchman®, Ellen Tracy®, Anne Klein®, Jones of New York®, and Stuart Wietzman® are leading examples of this style. Once you know what you're looking for, you can duplicate your style by shopping the name brands and stores in your area.

For Business
- ● You will rarely struggle to create a believable look with your choices for business attire. Make sure that you keep your "edge" by incorporating interesting new pieces and current accessories. (i.e. if tweeds are popular, add a tweed jacket)

Wardrobe tips / Do's and Don'ts
- ● Updating your accessories is one of the easiest ways to avoid the "rut" syndrome.
- ● Focus on keeping your look current and don't allow your clothes to age you before your time.
- ● Don't be guilty of buying the same item in different colors.

As a Modern Conservative, the daily disciplines of make-up application and styling your hair are important and often come naturally. Your pitfall can be spending too much time getting ready, which is just the opposite of the Practical Casual who usually likes low maintenance.

A Modern Conservative cares not only about how she presents herself but her surroundings are very important to her as well. At her dinner table you can bet there are place mats, matching silverware, and at least one candle lit for ambience.

A visible example in the media is Diane Sawyer of "Good Morning America."

Recipe

Great style is a result of consistently expressing who you are while feeling totally confident with the image you present.

The Risk Taker

Your Priority—Cutting edge fashion where style is preferred over comfort

A Risk Taker will have the *desire* as well as the *ability* to achieve and maintain the high fashion look.

Some or all of the following may apply:

- Shopping is your favorite activity.
- You dare to be different.
- You love clothes.
- You want the latest and the greatest in fashion and make-up.
- You enjoy being noticed for what you are wearing.
- Your hemlines go up and down with the trends.
- You love shoes and accessories.
- You are uninhibited.

Spin-offs of The Risk Taker:

The Dramatic
(striking, dramatic, sophisticated, and intimidating)

The Sexy
(enticing, alluring, passionate, sensual, glamorous)

The Artistic
(creative, original, imaginative, bohemian)

As a Risk Taker, you are always on a quest for the latest trends in clothes and accessories. You seek attention for your fashion statements. Whatever is the 'hot' look, you want to be in it!

Make-Up
Your make-up style will reflect the most current trends in application and color. Have fun discovering your favorite looks. Don't overdo it for business. Keep application less trendy and use the Modern Conservative approach to make-up.

Hairstyle
You change your style every time you get bored, which is usually every 3 to 4 months. Your hairstyle and color will reflect the latest trends. Keep it edgy but not wild or messy for business. If curly and/or long—control it.

Clothing Choices
Your clothing lines, hem lengths, fabrics, colors, patterns, details, and accessories will reflect the most current fashion trends. You will be constantly changing your look. Your style will usually be trendy, elaborate, striking, bold, and sometimes extreme.

Look for these stores and designers that cater to your style: Neiman Marcus®, Eileen Fisher®, Versace®, Vera Wang®, Fendi®, DKNY®. Once you know what you're looking for, you can duplicate your style by shopping the name brands and stores in your area.

For Business

- Be careful to dress appropriately for the occasion. You sometimes tend to be overdressed creating the focus on yourself instead of the business at hand. It will take some forethought before you get dressed everyday for business.

- Learn to put the controls on your choice of clothing for business. It is important to express your style but be approachable at the same time. Look more to the Modern Conservative for your clues to a successful business look.
- Wear a more conservative style and bring in cutting edge current accessory touches. (i.e. shoes, jewelry, handbags, etc.)
- To keep your appearance less intimidating, avoid extremes in your overall business look unless you're working in the fashion/arts industry.

Ruth's Seasoning

As a Risk Taker, I take a license to express myself and make a statement every chance I get! I spent almost 20 years of my life as an administrator for a large Midwest state university. A very professional environment set in a part of the country where it usually takes us about a year to catch on to current trends. Dressing as a Risk Taker I was always a square peg trying to fit in a round hole. I may have been on the cutting edge of fashion, but I often stood alone. Standing alone didn't bother me but the way my look alienated me from my peers did. People definitely *reacted* to me but did not *interact* with me. I made my statement! It was a statement that said I was not approachable. Every profession has a "uniform" and when we step too far away from the acceptable look we lose our value personally and professionally. I used to feel like I had to work extra hard at times to prove myself. As Risk Takers, we battle getting caught up in wanting to wear our latest "finds." Remember your goal as you choose your business wear. Save your latest "finds" for your social wardrobe.

A Risk Taker's lifestyle will usually reflect her clothing style. Her home may be extravagantly decorated like something in a storybook or out of a magazine. She loves to create events. Whether she's entertaining a few friends or throwing a big party, she will definitely make it a memorable experience for her guests. Her dinner table is often a "work of art" at the risk of not being able to actually sit down and enjoy a meal or see over the centerpiece to talk to the person on the other side of the table. Nothing about her is practical, but creating a beautiful environment for friends and family to enjoy is her gift.

A visible example in the media is Paula Abdul of "American Idol" fame.

Whether you found yourself relating to the *Practical Casual*, the *Modern Conservative*, or the *Risk Taker*, the more you know and understand about your style and what is right for you, the better you will feel in the clothes you choose. No longer will shopping trips have to be "hit or miss." You now have a recipe with directions that will help you get great results with your style. No more "fashion" mistakes. By narrowing your search, we have given you the freedom you need to make good buying decisions, to put more value to your clothing dollar, and to stop feeling guilty over bad decisions. Now go cook up your own style and have fun getting dressed every day!

Chapter
NINE

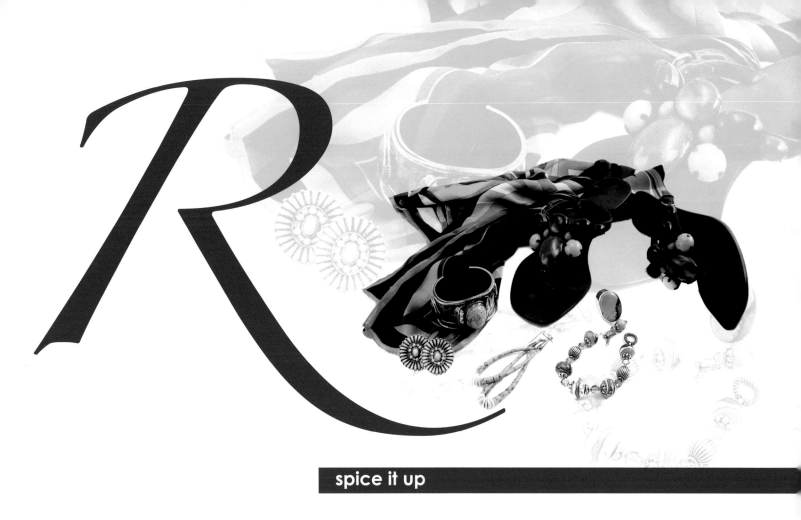

R

Wow! The overwhelming world of accessorizing! There are complete stores full of every kind of accessory under the sun. It's hard to know where to start. And with so much selection, how do we narrow down our choices to find the right shoes, handbags, scarves, pins, and hosiery that will complement our clothes? While it may seem like a daunting task, it can actually be a lot of fun.

The main purpose of accessorizing is to finish your look. It creates a positive impression by completing the whole picture. A picture that is complete and harmonized says, "I have it together. I can accomplish any

107

task, and I know what I am doing." Just as adding landscaping to a new house gives it "curb appeal," great accessorizing enhances your overall appeal making you more approachable. Though on the inside, there isn't one of us who isn't a "work in progress", looking our very best conveys to others that we are committed to putting our best foot forward.

Aside from finishing your look, accessorizing is another wonderful avenue to expressing your unique individuality. It's just like spaghetti. While we may all make the same dish, adding different spices sets our flavor apart from the rest. Some spices add richness, while others add zest. Some spices are bold, while others are subtle. And like spices, our accessories can also add versatility to the clothes we wear by creating different looks for the same outfit. So, rather than having the same old spaghetti time after time, we can make it spicy some days, and sweet on other days. And if our recipe is starting to taste a little old and outdated, rather than throwing it out altogether, we can simply add fresh basil to create a whole new taste. Like the old saying goes, variety is the spice of life!

To Accessorize or Not? . . . That is the question!

Many times you will find clothing that is already accessorized with patterns, colors, textures, buttons, contrasting stitching, or trim. The accessorizing, or lack of it, in your clothing is what will determine what you do with your add-on accessories like shoes, handbags, jewelry, and hosiery. It determines whether you make your accessories a focal point or a finishing point. Your clothes and accessories are meant to *complement* each other, *not compete* for attention! The more elaborate in size and detail your accessories become, the simpler your clothes need to be.

Accessories are what set you apart from everyone else.

Your Style Signature

Think of accessories as the signature to your style. Consider what kind of an impression you want to leave with people. Whether you want to convey that you are professional, casual, sassy, conservative, fun, or anything else, your signature can help you to accomplish your unique style. Here are a few general guidelines to start with when making your selections:

- Your accessories should express your style and fit the mood or theme of your outfit.
- Don't put yourself in a "matchy-matchy" box—go for harmony and balance. Everything doesn't *have* to match.
- Less is more.
- Have only one focal point.
- Avoid extremes. Steer clear of too flashy or too plain.
- "If in doubt . . . don't!" Choose accessories that are appropriate for the location, season, and occasion.
- Use accessories to draw attention away from figure challenges. For example, if hips are large, place accessories as focal points above the waist.
- The size of your accessories should be in balance with your body.
- Save enough of your clothing budget to finish the outfit with accessories.

Now, let's take a look at the different types of accessories we wear and how we can make the right selections that will complement our clothes and create our unique *style signature*.

The Power of SHOES

There is a store close to my home that has a sign that I just love. It says, "DANGER! SHOE SALE." I don't know about you, but shoes have a special power over me and it takes little to persuade me to purchase a new pair. Women never seem to have enough shoes or too many! But as much as we love shoes, we often make the mistake of thinking that since they are worn – well, all the way "down there," no one will really notice if they don't harmonize with our clothes or look all that great. We are wrong. In fact, the exact opposite is true.

The first place we need to spend our money when investing in accessories is shoes. Shoe styles change as often as clothing styles do and heel and toe shapes will date our shoes very quickly. Shoes also lend personality to your outfit. No matter what your preferred clothing style may be, your shoes should be one of the first considerations when making accessory purchases.

Get the most bang for your buck!

How you spend your money on shoes will be very important. In the Midwest, I only get to wear sandals about 3 months out of the year so it just doesn't make sense for me to spend a lot of money on sandals. And as a Risk Taker, I buy the trends that will be "over" by next year. So, rather than buying expensive sandals, I choose to invest in shoes I will wear more often.

If you are like me and you buy very trendy shoes, don't spend a lot. They won't be around long enough to justify it. The same goes for special occasion shoes. You may only wear these once or twice so don't empty your purse in order to buy them. A classic style shoe, on the other hand, is likely to remain in style for up to 4 or more seasons so your money will be well spent on a higher quality shoe that will last.

If you have challenges with your feet that require good shoes, this is not a place to "skimp." Be good to your feet and invest in the right shoes. Don't sacrifice your feet to fit into a more stylish shoe either. Your feet will thank you and you will also prevent more serious problems down the road.

Remember, you are trying to make a great impression so give careful consideration to the occasion and type of outfit you will be wearing before you give in to the impulse to buy that "Oh, so cute" pair of shoes that you can't live without. The exception would be if you have unlimited funds to spend and can buy both the *irresistible* pair and the *needed* pair to complete a couple of outfits that you frequently wear.

- Always take note of two features: toe and heel shape.
- Watch the trends and update last year's outfits with a current shoe choice.
- Unusual heel shapes will date shoes very quickly so keep this in mind when considering your purchase.

Recipe

Shoes are one of the first things people notice.

Does the shoe fit the occasion and look of your outfit?

- When wearing heavier fabrics and covering more of the body, choose a heavier, more closed in shoe. *Example*: A heavy wool suit or winter fabric skirt and sweater should be worn with a closed toe shoe or boot.
- For lighter weight fabrics where more of the body is open and exposed, choose a lighter, more open shoe. *Example*: A dress of light or airy fabric should be worn with a strappy or sandal style heel, high or low.
- Different occasions require different shoes. *Example*: If you are a business professional, you need a professional shoe or boot with the business look you will wear to the office. This requires a style with a slight heel and no chunky or strappy looks. Casual occasion shoes will range from flats, to sandals, to chunky shoes when in style and sneakers. Your dressy shoes may have some glitter or shine to them and can be strappy. Just remember, these looks are not appropriate for the office.

Shoes are key to keeping your look current!

Choose shoes that will flatter your body frame.

Shoe styles will change with every season bringing a variety of heel heights, toe shapes, and heel shapes. Not all styles will be flattering on every body. The principles of proportion for creating balance that we have shared throughout the book when referring to the prints you wear, the details on an item, and your accessories, will also ring true with your shoes. Keep in mind the following when choosing styles:

- Medium to high heels elongate legs and improve calf shape.
- Heavy legs should avoid extremes in heels—thick or thin.
- Very square toes make most legs look shorter or heavier.
- Classic round, square round, or slightly pointed toes are great for every leg.
- Very pointed toes are sexy, dramatic, and elongating to both foot and leg.
- Ankle straps are not good for thick legs.
- Chunky shoes will not be flattering on thick legs.
- Avoid very high heels if you are petite.
- Larger body frames should avoid dainty, skimpy style shoes.

Keep your shoes in good shape!

It is very important to pay attention to the "shape" your shoes are in and keep them looking good. It is so easy to put them on, day after day, and not notice the gradual wear and tear. But others *will* notice! So, make a conscious effort to take care of your shoes.

- Clean or polish regularly.
- Use water repellent spray to protect against water damage for leather shoes.
- Don't wear the same shoes everyday; give them a rest in between.
- Send old worn out shoes to "shoe heaven."

Handbags

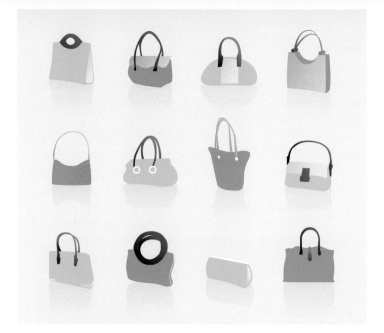

Handbags have gone from function to FUN. These days they truly are an accessory that adds value to your appearance . . . and not just when there's money in them!

Here are a few tips for choosing a great handbag:

- Keep it current!
- Choose a bag that is proportioned to the size of your body for the best look. In other words, if you're 5'2", carrying a great big bag that looks like it takes both hands just to get it on your shoulder . . . it's not your best choice.
- For a casual/relaxed look—carry an unstructured soft leather/fabric bag.
- For a professional look—carry a medium sized bag with more structure. Surface should be smooth with clean, simple details.
- For a dressy/evening look—carry a small to medium shiny, beaded, or fabric bag.

Your handbag doesn't have to match your shoes, but it should go with your overall look.

Hosiery

Today's fashion statement has changed when it comes to hosiery. For years the big question was, "What color hosiery should I wear?" Now it's, "Do I really *need* to wear hosiery?" As a result, younger women may feel "behind the times" wearing hosiery while many older women don't feel right without it. Regardless of your generation, in the more conservative, professional occupations, hosiery is, and always will be, a must. For more casual work settings and special occasions, however, hosiery is a matter of preference and your choice will depend on the look you want to achieve.

If you want to go without hosiery, keep in mind you will be showing off your legs, so consider first what they look like. You really shouldn't go bare legged unless you have a smooth and somewhat tanned leg. Use a self-tanner to add a little color to your legs, and at the same time, hide minor flaws with a concealer or foundation to give them a smoother look. If your legs just don't tolerate going bare then you can have a bare leg look by wearing a soft, natural sheer hosiery shade.

Now, if you're thinking to yourself, "But I hate wearing hose! They run, sag at the ankles, snag, have tight waistbands, and hang in the crotch." It may be because you've been wearing the wrong hose. Well, you don't have to! Hosiery can be comfortable and last longer if you remember two key things: Lycra is the magic ingredient! Buying your correct size and style makes a big difference.

A word to the wise—buying a good pair of hose can be expensive, but in the long run, you will save money by purchasing longer-lasting, better-looking hose. By the time you add up the amount spent replacing cheaper pairs of hose, you could have just purchased one good pair that will last longer if you take care of them!

And whether you wear hose everyday or just occasionally, watch the fashion reports for current colors, textures, and weights. Be aware of trends and stay current. For example, in the late 90s matching your color of hosiery with the color of your outfit was very stylish. More recently, a natural color leg has been the trend. Whatever the trend, always complement your hosiery shade to your clothing.

Flattering Fit for Eyes

Do you know that if you wear glasses, they are your most important accessory? And you thought they were just an "opto-pedic" appliance! Think about it. They are worn on your face in front of your most important feature, your eyes, on a daily basis. So, instead of hiding behind them, show off who you are and enhance your features with a great pair of frames.

When choosing a frame consider the following:

Is the style, shape, and size current?

Size is the key to staying current. Size range, if current, will tell people whether or not you know what year or decade you are in. Medium size frames are the safest. They will stay current longer than large or small frames. To be fashionable, look at the current frames being displayed and choose accordingly. Realize that your frames will need to be changed every couple of years, not five or ten! This is especially true as you age. Don't think you have to give up that perfectly good, but slightly outdated pair of frames. Recycle them—have the lenses tinted and wear them as sunglasses or donate them.

Does the style, shape, and size enhance my features?

Styles, shapes, and sizes that flatter/enhance your facial features should always be considered, unless fashion dictates otherwise. Frame shape should create a sense of balance with your features, not mirror your face shape. In other words, choose a wider frame to balance out a wide jaw-line and choose an angular frame to offset a rounded face. Eyebrows should be complemented by the frame shape and not necessarily covered up. Smaller frames will sit below the eyebrow. The color of your frames should flatter your skin tone and hair color and work with your wardrobe. CAUTION: Rimless style frames can be aging if you are over 40 and your hair is gray.

Do they fit?

Your frames don't fit correctly if you are pushing them back into place every 5 minutes! A good fit is crucial. Be sure to get your frames fitted by a professional and have them adjusted every few months as needed. For a clean, fresh look, replace old yellow nose pads. Most places offer this as a complimentary service.

We are going to wear our glass frames in more situations than probably any other accessory we own. We will wear them whether dressed up or down, at home or the office, for special occasions, ball games, and PTA meetings. Do you think one pair of glass frames will do it? Would one pair of shoes be enough? Of course not! No one frame does it all, so invest in two pair of glass frames to achieve a great look for every occasion.

Jewelry

A simple diamond studded bracelet, a real strand of pearls, or a gold watch can be a wonderful way to finish your look. However, wearing *fashion jewelry* gives us the chance to express who we are and enjoy many different looks. Whether you want simple, extravagant, or somewhere in between, costume jewelry can fit your look because it comes in all different shapes, sizes, colors, themes, and many times can be great imitations of the real thing. So have fun with it!

Jewelry can be a very versatile accessory used as a focal point or simply a finishing point. Jazz up that basic black dress or add a simple final touch to a colorful jacket. I often choose jewelry to change the look of an outfit, dressing it up or making it more casual. One of the most effective ways to use jewelry is to update your wardrobe inexpensively by adding the latest style earrings, necklaces, bracelets, or pins. With so many options, it's easy to get out of control with jewelry. Here are a few simple guidelines that will give you the freedom to enjoy your fashion jewelry.

Recipe

My husband gave me a necklace. It's fake. I requested fake. Maybe I'm paranoid, but in this day and age, I don't want something around my neck that's worth more than my head.

~Rita Rudner

Jewelry Do's and Don'ts:

1. Accessorize your ears first if nothing else.

2. A necklace can be an easy place to make a mistake so consider the following:
   - Is the outfit already accessorized with details? If so, don't add a necklace!
   - Does the outfit really need it or are you just adding it for the heck of it? Less is more.
   - Does your necklace complement your neckline or does it look out of place?
     For example: avoid wearing a collarless v-neckline with a necklace that drops lower then the opening of the neck. Your necklace should be short enough to fill in the neckline. Try to avoid wearing a short necklace with a high round neckline because it will compete with the neckline rather than complement it.

3. When it comes to a long necklace, don't wear one that ends at your bust or it will bounce and swing in the air as you walk.

4. Choker necklaces look best on average to long necks.

5. If you like to wear a lot of jewelry, keep your outfit "quieter" to show off the jewelry.

6. Jewelry should be proportionate to the size of your body and facial features.

7. Jewelry pieces do not have to match, but should coordinate.

8. Pins should be placed 3-4 inches down from the top of your shoulder, not worn at bust line level.

9. If you are not a jewelry person, get a great pair of sterling silver or 14K gold small hoops, put them in, and forget them.

10. Be courteous to those around you; avoid jewelry with too much ringing, clanging, or rattling. Consider the occasion. For business, jewelry should always be seen, but not heard!

Applying perfume or hairspray with jewelry on can damage it permanently.

If you are a *Practical Casual*, minimal accessories will most likely be your preference. You should focus on a good pair of shoes, a handbag, and one versatile pair of earrings. If you are a *Modern Conservative*, you enjoy accessories, so what we have shared will guide you as you choose your favorites. Finally, if you are a *Risk Taker*, it is important that you pay particular attention to following the guidelines for business settings in order not to sabotage your business goals. But in your own personal time, it's all you baby!

Recipe

The most important thing to remember when accessorizing is to STAY CURRENT!

Chapter
TEN

what's in the pantry?

Over the years, I've learned that a well-organized pantry always contributes to the success of a recipe. Knowing what's in the pantry *always* makes a big difference. It's helps me know which ingredients I will need when making my shopping list, helps me discover what items are expired (without finding out the hard way), and saves time and frustration when preparing a recipe because I can easily locate and grab what I need. Just like the pantry, knowing what's in your closet and getting it organized will help make this *Recipe for Your Best Personal Style* a success.

123

Wouldn't you love to start your day with a totally organized closet? Imagine waking up in the morning and being able to grab an outfit from the hanger—not the bottom of the laundry basket—and have it look great on the first try. What a concept! We've all had those frustrating days when nothing we choose seems to work.

Here's a familiar scene: Laurie stands in front of her closet anticipating the different roles she'll play for the day. First, she'll get the kids to school and volunteer in her son's 2nd grade class for a few hours. Next, she's off to a lunch meeting with some new clients before heading back to school to pick up the kids and drop them off at soccer practice. She'll then run home to make dinner and do a few loads of laundry before leaving the kids with dad to head off to the PTA meeting.

Hmmm . . . what should she wear? She slips on her black pants that have always been so reliable. Nope! Those 5 extra pounds she put on over the holidays have just ruled out that option. Okay, the gray suit should work. But she never did get around to getting the pants hemmed. Now what? One after another, Laurie pulls things out of her closet as the pile of "un-wearables" on her bed grows bigger and bigger. The pink blouse? No. The two-piece knit? Too casual. Those olive green pants she just had to buy? Nothing to go with them. She finally settles on the same old navy pants with the boring taupe top and leaves the house feeling defeated. Can you relate?

Recipe

Simplify your life by organizing your closet.

124

Clean out your closet at least once a year.

We need to clean out our closets at least once a year, not only to be more organized, but also to simplify our lives. This will allow us to evaluate how our needs may have changed over the year and what we may be hanging on to that needs to go. If you haven't worn something in a year, chances are you never will. It's just taking up space.

Start by taking *everything*, yes *everything*, out of your closet. Just like an artist, we need to start with a clean canvas.

Make 3 different piles:

The **first pile** will be things to give away. You know which ones I mean, the ones you haven't worn in at least a year. Maybe it worked in the eighties and you're waiting for the fad to come back again. If it doesn't fit, looks worn, has a stain, or belongs on someone 20 years younger, or 20 years older than you, toss it! When in doubt—it's out!

Now, let's work with what we have left. Make a **second pile** of the things that need attention. Is it over-due for the dry cleaners? Does it need to be hemmed, altered, or just a little TLC? Shoes that need polish, something with a missing button, or the skirt that you love, but still needs to be taken in (or out) goes here.

The **third pile** will be the keepers. Remember the 80/20 rule? It's so true. We have a closet jam packed of everything, from our prom dress to the 13 "work in the yard" t-shirts and everything in between. Yet, we gravitate to the same 20%, so put the 20% you wear in this pile. These are the items we feel great in. Once it's on, we can forget about it. If it's "your color", fits great, feels comfortable, or you get compliments when you have it on, chances are it's a keeper.

Be sure to follow through with getting rid of your *first pile*, giving proper attention to your *second pile*, and as you begin to put the keepers back in the closet from your *third pile*, focus on getting them organized.

Closet Secrets

- If you can't see it you won't wear it. Your clothes should be spaced so you can see the sleeve or leg of every item. Clean it out completely before organizing it or going shopping.
- Whether plastic, wood, or metal, use uniform hangers and hang everything by length: pants, skirts, shorts, jackets, tops, shirts, dresses, etc.
- Keep similar items together. Group by piece and then by color—jeans together, pants together, skirts together, etc.—then jeans by color, blue, black, brown, etc.
- Fold sweaters and heavy items and store in clear containers that are visible on the shelf. Store vintage items (old favorites) in another closet or place—even in a box under your bed.
- Store shoes on a shoe rack or in plastic, see through boxes. If you are lucky enough to have built in shoe storage, you can rearrange them there.
- Consider closet accessories like belt racks, hooks for organizing your outfits for the week, and multi-pocket organizers for jewelry, hosiery, and accessories.
- Organizer "experts" will tell you that every time you buy something to add to your closet you should also get rid of something. Give it a try and see if it works for you.

Just thinking about getting organized feels really great and I bet you can't wait to get to it! When you're done, sit back and give yourself a pat on the back. You will have completely simplified your life and getting dressed every day won't be a hassle.

Chapter
ELEVEN

shopping list

We have a handle on what colors to gravitate toward, we've cleaned out our closet, and we also have some key points to looking great. Now we can make a shopping list. What should you focus on during the upcoming shopping trip? It's tempting to be like a six year old at Christmas making his list to Santa, but let me remind you: Never go in debt to buy new clothes!

If money is tight, there are some resources available to you. Your best bet is to head for the consignment shop, discount store, or even a thrift store where the deals are to be found. You may be thinking, "Thrift store? You're kidding right?" Well, no. I've found some complete "gems" in those places and you can too if you're up for the hunt. If you hate shopping, I suggest heading to the mall during the sales seasons to save some money. Most importantly, plan ahead and stick to your list so you are not sabotaged by "those great buys" for the sake of saving money! Now, with a renewed sense of clarity and purpose, it's time to go shopping!

For those of us who were born to shop, we can't imagine missing out on that amazing "find" at the 1/2 off yearly sale. Our motto is, "If the shoe fits, buy it!" But let's face it, not all of us were born to shop. Some of us "non-shoppers" would much rather make do with what's already in the closet than to brave the department store.

Why is it that even the most experienced of shoppers can get discouraged at times? Here are some reasons:

- Too many choices in the stores.
- Several looks going on all at the same time in fashion.
- Confusion over what to wear to an event.
- An unclear idea what styles are best for us.
- A lack of options available in our best colors.
- Inability to find a great fit.
- The struggle to stay within a budget.
- Fear of spending too much time with no results.

Recipe

If you're not a "shopper", bring a friend with you who is one.

If you are a non-shopper, you will be most successful by working with two to three core items (pants, skirts, jackets) and focusing on buying complementary pieces. You will get too overwhelmed if you have to come up with a whole outfit at one time, unless you see items grouped together at the store on a hanger. Stores like Stein Mart put a great deal into marketing their merchandise using this method. Unfortunately, non-shoppers almost never succeed at discount stores like TJ Maxx, Marshals, or Ross where it takes a savvier shopper to put together outfits from the hodgepodge of clothing styles and sizes available. While places like these are excellent stores for a shopper, it takes way too much time, energy, and patience for a non-shopper to sort through the masses to find a look. Here's where a "shopper" friend could be of real help. She'll love pulling pieces for you that go together and she'll feel like she has contributed something while getting the thrill of shopping without spending her own money.

We all know that a "shopper" has no problem shopping. Like the non-shopper, she has her own set of problems. She tends to over buy. It's a form of recreation. She buys because: It is such a good deal. She's attracted to what is new. Shopping is an addiction. She can't go to a store without buying something.

The shopper often over spends on herself and even goes into debt because of the "I just can't live without that certain something" syndrome. Her greatest problem is that she has no plan and ends up with a hodgepodge of looks. She has too many clothes with the tags still on because she has nowhere to wear them or nothing to coordinate. She can't seem to put her look together consistently and usually ends up wearing something once and then not liking how it makes her feel. Ever been there? Me too.

Another difference between a non-shopper and a shopper is that a non-shopper will repeat a favorite item in a different color because she gets into a rut. Four different "flavors" of the same top works great for her. On the other hand, the shopper is ready to move on to the next look, sometimes too quickly as if she is on a safari looking for the next big hunt.

If you are a non-shopper, you may want to hire a professional or take along a fashion savvy friend. Whether you are a shopper or a non-shopper, you can be successful and the following information will give you the knowledge to make your purchases with confidence.

Let's look at what makes a successful purchase:

- You feel good in it.
- People compliment you when you wear it.
- It fits well over all.
- It is comfortable.
- You are not self-conscious about your body flaws in it.
- It fits your need and the occasion.
- It is a favorite color.

Here are a few things to remember, if you want to like and wear what you buy:

1. Don't shop in a hurry.

2. Don't buy something just because you are attracted to it. Ask yourself these questions:
    - Do I have anything to wear it with?
    - Where will I wear it? Does it fit my wardrobe needs?
    - How often will I wear it? Is it comfortable?

3. Don't buy something on sale if you would not buy it at retail. It's so tempting, but try to refrain.

4. You must try it on wearing the right undergarments.

5. Evaluate the style and fit. Be sure it fits and looks great standing, sitting, and from behind.

6. Be objective—remember many great outfits do not always have hanger appeal.

7. Don't be too size conscious! Remember, at least 50% of all women wear a plus size somewhere on their body and 14 is the average size a buyer purchases. So, check your attitude about sizing at the dressing room door. What matters most is how it fits and that you find something that looks and feels good on you. In fact, if the size tags bother you that much when you see them in your closet, *cut them out!*

8. Consider the following before heading out on your shopping adventure:
    - Moderately priced clothing is usually cut smaller than more expensive items.
    - Clothing designs change from season to season.
    - Are you choosing your clothes from the right departments?

Stop and think it through before making that impulse purchase.

Plan ahead for a time when you will not be rushed, to head out on your shopping excursion. It's very tempting to buy that "What was I thinking?" item when you're in a hurry. So, grab your *shopping list* and make a day of it . . . okay, an afternoon, and enjoy.

Chapter
TWELVE

K

microwave style

As I was strolling with my grocery cart through the produce section, I noticed a familiar face. One of the moms from my son's school was stocking up for the week. She smiled at me and said, "You even look put together at the grocery store! How do you do it? With little kids at home, I'm lucky to get my hair brushed and my sweats on." I could totally relate. The fact is that I probably didn't spend a whole lot more time getting ready in the morning than she did.

137

The mad dash out the door to get kids to school is probably a familiar one if you have children. Once breakfast is served, the lunches made, kids dressed, hair done, teeth brushed, etc. . . . the clock is ticking away and it's so tempting to say, "Forget it!" when it comes to looking even the least bit put together.

Our time is so valuable. Most of us would say that if given the choice, a cold sandwich would take second place to a hot, home cooked meal any day. Although, there IS the microwave and you can prepare some great meals in 15 minutes. I've noticed that what can make those quick meals successful is: they require limited ingredients, there are no complicated or time-consuming steps, they don't require an hour in the oven, and they incorporate a little pre-planning.

Whether you are a business executive or a domestic engineer, looking put together doesn't have to take second place to "At least I got my hair brushed." We have a microwave style recipe with some basic guidelines that you can follow to feel great about yourself when you start your day. And it doesn't have to take you an hour! Who has the time? Set the timer for 15 minutes and be ready to step out the door looking great when the buzzer goes off.

Put Your Best Face Forward

It's fun to read through the make-up chapter and learn all of the steps to a *finished* face. Can't you just picture yourself with all the time in the world, enjoying every one of the steps, from concealer to lip liner, loose powder to brow pencil? But come on, it just isn't a reality for many of us.

A great look doesn't mean that you have to have a full face of make-up. If your skin is clean and fresh, that's a wonderful place to start. If you don't have one already, add a skin care routine to your schedule. It gives you a healthy glow and keeps your skin looking younger. We all want that!

A "finished" look shouldn't take more than 5 minutes to accomplish.

Just a few items of make-up can give you that fresh, put together, finished look. Here are the essentials:

- Powder Foundation
- Mascara
- A touch of Blush
- Lip Gloss

Have a Great Haircut

Having a great haircut doesn't necessarily mean you have to have short hair. If you choose to wear your hair longer, just make sure it has style. When you're short on time, it's very tempting to pull it back in a ponytail. Instead, find fun clips or a headband to dress up your look. Plan on visiting your hair stylist every 6 weeks and try something different. You'll feel like a new person!

Comfort?!

Many people today have taken comfort to a whole new level. An oversized, wrinkled cotton t-shirt and sweat pants should be worn for yard work, not outings. This doesn't mean that you have to sacrifice comfort. There are plenty of great looking, comfortable sweat suits, jeans, and YES, even tennis shoes.

Remember this. You don't know who you're going to run into. It never fails! When you go on that quick errand and think you won't see anyone you know, a familiar face comes walking up. So instead of hearing, "Tough day?" Make it, "You look really great today!"

My friend, Pam, is married with two wonderful young boys and works for an eye doctor processing claims. Like all busy moms, she is constantly struggling to find enough time in the day for all that needs to be done. Over the years, I've spent many hours listening to her agonize over wanting to be the best at her job while being a loving wife, attentive mother, and still maintaining a sense of herself. "It can't be done!" she would say. "I'm such a failure." I'm sure we can all relate to that feeling at one point or another. All of us have obligations and it's easy to neglect ourselves at times in order to try and live up to the expectations we've placed on ourselves. It doesn't have to be that way.

I want to give you a few time saving tips that will allow you the luxury of choosing to spend a few extra minutes on yourself. When you only have 15 minutes in the morning to get out the door, you won't have to decide what is more important . . . hair and make-up or dishes, getting the kids to school with lunch and books in hand, and being at work on time. You can do it all and look great too!

- Decide what tasks can be done the night before to simplify your morning.
- Keep your closet ready.
- Organize five to seven outfits for the week.
- Keep grooming essentials at your fingertips.
- For a fast exit, have a blow and go hairstyle.
- Don't leave the house with wet hair.

Chapter
THIRTEEN

just like wine, better with time

Have you had that continual 29th birthday yet? Is 40 looming on the horizon? Your 25-year high school reunion is just around the corner? You just qualified for the senior discount on American Airlines? AARP is sending you renewal notices? The phrase, "Help, I've fallen and I can't get up," isn't so funny anymore? Unfortunately, there is no cure for aging. I love what Mark Twain said, "Age is an issue of mind over matter. If you don't mind, it doesn't matter." And it shouldn't matter. Every day we are blessed to have a new beginning and it is a gift to treasure. Remember that age brings with it maturity and wisdom to offer to younger generations.

However, even if we're at peace with aging, no woman wants to appear older than she is. An entire industry thrives on our desire to defy the signs of aging. We snatch up the magazines in the check out aisle to read the articles promising to help us look 10 years younger if we use their new make-up techniques, specialized exercise routine, or age defying supplement. TV and radio advertisements are continually promoting the latest gadget, exercise equipment, cosmetic surgery, and spa services that can bring back our youthful appearance. And if all else fails, we could just have a complete overhaul like they do on those "extreme makeover" shows.

When it comes to staying young, a mind-lift beats a face-lift any day.   ~ Marty Bucella

How realistic is that though? Whether it's lack of funds, time, or even aversion to pain, that type of treatment isn't in the future for most of us. What is the answer? First of all, we've got to look at our body as a whole. Women tend to break up their bodies and focus, big time, on the negative instead of the positive. We've all been there. Just look in a full-length mirror and our eyes are drawn to the problem areas.

And why shouldn't we? We're comparing ourselves to the fortunate ones who are put before us day after day in the media. You know the ones, "She's 50, but she has the body of a 35 year old. And if you use the same exercise equipment that she does, you can look just like her." Yeah, right! This woman is a model who "works out" for a living, not to mention the great genes she's inherited.

My body doesn't really compare. Yet without fail, whenever I travel back to a familiar group of people at a seminar, individuals come to me and say, "You look younger every time I see you. How do you do it?" I believe there are several reasons that I get comments like that. And, unlike that exercise equipment, these are things that I know you can realistically apply to your own image.

- Choose to use great skin care faithfully, twice a day.
- Make-up helps! Keep application age appropriate and flattering.
- Assess your hairstyle at least once a year. Keep it current and flattering. Never miss that 4 to 6 week visit to the salon.
- Alter hair color to keep a youthful appearance. Keep hair color changes in harmony with your skin undertone. You may need to lighten hair color that's too dark, or add some depth of color to blonde hair that's so pale it washes you out.
- Keep working on posture and body language. Physical exercise is key. There are many kinds of exercise, from swimming to walking, exercises with deep breathing to Pilates, even aerobics. Find and commit to what works for you.
- Change your self-talk. Stop talking to yourself about what parts of your body you hate. There are things we would all like to change, but hey, there is only so much we can do! Let's stop being obsessed with the "not so great" parts.
- Focus on what assets you do have and play them up with the right accessories, clothing lines, hairstyle, and make-up.

Recipe

The process of maturing is an art to be learned, an effort to be sustained. By the age of fifty you have made yourself what you are, and if it's good, it's better than your youth.

~ Marya Mannes, More in Anger, 1958

145

The following are some fashion "Do's" to help you age with energy and keep that youthful appearance:

- You should always softly define your body, but avoid too soft or clingy fabrics because they can make the body look dumpy and they also have a tendency to cling to bulges or sagging areas. We definitely don't want that!
- Use more structured garments because they make the body look more youthful and trim.
- Alter clothes to fit your body. At each stage of our lives our bodies change and our clothing needs to change accordingly.
- Don't be defeated by changing body and figure challenges. Focus on solutions and learn to adapt. The good news is that 80% of it can be camouflaged.
- Stay current with fashion and update your look . . .
  If hoop earrings or chandelier earrings are "in", choose a moderate version of them to wear.
  If you like to wear scarves, wear them only if the style is a current look.
- Update your shoes. Find the ones that provide the comfort and fit you require, BUT are also stylish and not aging.
- Glass frames are key to a youthful look. Choose a defined frame with an edgy look that is not too dark or strong for your face.

Don't get into a rut with your clothing or hairstyles. It will age you.

When we use the correct visual tools, we send the correct message. And remember, it takes a complete picture to enjoy the visual results.

Janie, who was waiting to have knee replacement surgery, told me that she was not interested in clothes. She implied that there were more important things to focus on than what clothes to wear. At the time, Janie was around 50 lbs. overweight and knowing that she would be inactive for several weeks after her surgery, made a decision to lose the weight. I was very hopeful for her and she was taking a definite step in the right direction.

To a degree, I could understand how Janie felt because there certainly are more important things in life than the clothes we wear. But at the same time, I also knew the significant impact that our appearance has on the important things in our lives.

A few months later, when I saw Janie again, I couldn't have been more pleasantly surprised. Not only had she lost weight, she had a new current and sassy hairstyle, and she looked great. She told me that she had gone shopping and had some great help at the store where she ended up purchasing some new coordinating clothes. Not only could I see a difference, I could *feel* the difference just talking with her. She now oozed confidence, had a bounce in her step, and was joyfully receiving compliments on how "youthful" and great she looked!

Just as Janie discovered, it is often our exterior that sparks the dramatic changes in how we feel, not necessarily the other way around. Whether you currently feel great about yourself or not, *you can* look and feel better! Just start by taking those little baby steps or giant steps in the direction of the changes you felt led to take.

My goal for each of you is that you would make those changes and become a more youthful, or (in some cases) more mature, healthier, and happier you. And remember, just as wine gets better with age, we, as women, do too!

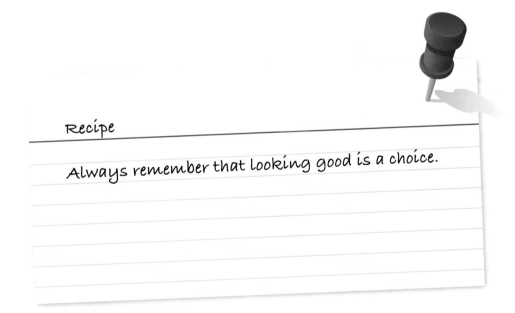

Recipe

Always remember that looking good is a choice.

Unfortunately, in today's society we are witnessing a gradual lowering of standards in the way we dress. It's like a recipe gone very wrong and you certainly wouldn't want to serve it to the ones you love. Some leave very little to the imagination! Kind of leaves a "bad taste" in your mouth. Pride and values need to be instilled into our youth today more than ever.

When it comes to looking good it is simply a choice that you must make. Pay attention to the important details that affect how others will perceive you. Excuses, like lack of money or time, may be robbing you of the opportunity to feel better, confident, and more capable of connecting with others. Little things truly can make a big difference. Apply this *Recipe For Your Best Personal Style* and make it one you can pass down from generation to generation.

Chapter
FOURTEEN

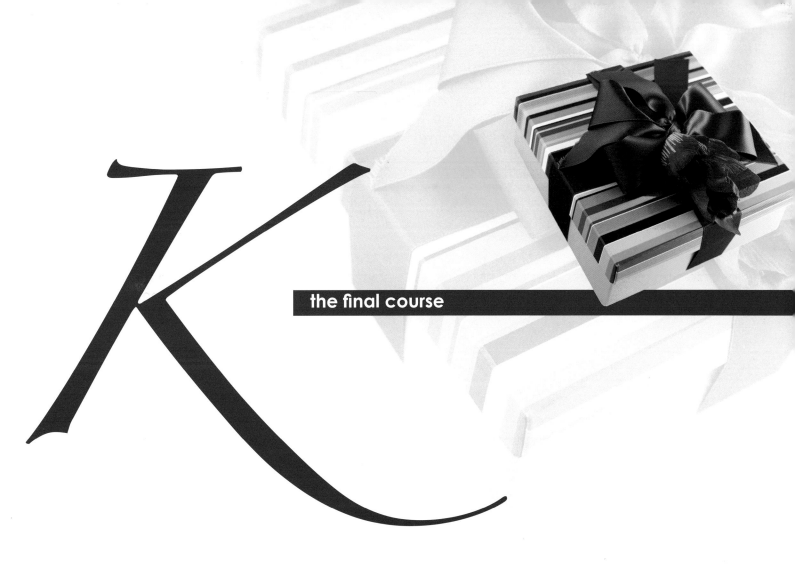

the final course

Have you ever received a really beautifully wrapped gift? I can still recall a particular gift I received that was covered with a pink, purple, and cream striped paper. The thick satin ribbon matched the purple perfectly and it had a special fresh, matching flower tied on top. Wow, was I impressed! The presentation was gift enough—I didn't even want to open it. I could tell just by the wrapping that whatever was in that special gift was going to be amazing! Like a gift, our presentation is a set of "cues and clues" as to what's inside, and people will draw conclusions about who we are based on those clues.

Don't you think it's time to give yourself a gift? Have you ever thought about an "extreme makeover"? The popularity of makeover shows was incredible. We sat and watched, wishing we were the ones getting the royal treatment, and the truth is we can all look and feel great without going on a TV show or having major cosmetic surgery.

My friend Jennifer is a perfect example of how anyone can make a change. Jen is one of those wonderful people who gives, gives, gives and never expects anything in return. Happy being in the background, she's never been one to make a fuss over how she looks. I decided I wanted to make Jen feel as special as she makes everyone else feel and convinced her to come and be pampered. We started by giving Jen a complete facial. Her skin was glowing! Next, we went through the color drapes and showed her all of the shades that would complement her beautiful brown hair and flawless olive skin. She told me she felt like a queen as I used cosmetics to enhance all of her great features.

Partly because an extra 20 pounds of post baby weight, Jen had never felt comfortable in clothes that would show off her curvy figure. She had a tendency to wear large, bulky sweaters or oversized sweatshirts with outdated jeans to cover up and she admitted that she needed to update her wardrobe. After trying some different styles, we found a pair of stylish, wide leg jeans and a great knit top from her color palette. Some cute sandals and a few perfectly placed accessories were the finishing touches. Wow!

Finally, we stopped in the salon for a complete new hairstyle and eyebrow shaping. My dear friend was being transformed before my eyes. I couldn't help but notice her confidence growing. When the last curl was in place, Jen's salon chair was turned to face the mirror and this wonderful woman who gives so much to others, burst into tears. "I never thought I could look this beautiful."

A flood of emotions came from years of insecurities, low self-esteem, and feelings of shame because of her weight. Jen's inner attitude was reflected in her baggy clothes and a no fuss look she chose for herself. This sweet, wonderful, caring woman was hiding behind the lie that she didn't care about how she looked and wasn't worth the time and effort. This was just a simple makeover day...nothing extreme, except the change in Jen's attitude about who she is. A beautiful woman!

I encourage you to make peace with your body. Accept the things you cannot change and change the things you can. It will make it much easier to "do life" on an everyday basis. Be the person that God created you to be! Your value doesn't come from the body you have but from knowing that you are loved and valued.

The way we present ourselves is a gift to those around us.

Have you heard, "Beauty comes from the inside"? We've covered so much in this book—from what colors to wear, to organizing your closet, and everything in between. You can have it all together on the outside and still be an unhappy person. You can have the outside all wrong and be the most beautiful person there is on the inside. It's a choice, not something you're born with. Why not have the best of both?

In this fast paced, instant gratification world we live in we have got to take some time to reflect. I've learned this. When I start my day with some quiet time, things go a whole lot better. Why not wake up an extra 15 minutes early and read from an inspirational book, do some deep breathing, write your thoughts in a journal, or simply reflect on all the gifts in your life. Your outer beauty will be enhanced by the inner beauty and peace this time will bring you.

An "extreme makeover" *is* attainable by simply following the guidelines in this book, and it won't cost you thousands of dollars. Take what you've learned and apply it in your life. Appreciate who you are, realize you were created beautiful, and decide that it's time to reveal that beauty and share it with the world. Give yourself and those you love a wonderful gift—the gift of the best you! You CAN do it and you're worth it! Start cooking up *A Recipe for Your Best Personal Style* . . . and Enjoy!